**THE DARWEN COUNTY
HISTORY SERIES**

A History of
HUNTINGDONSHIRE

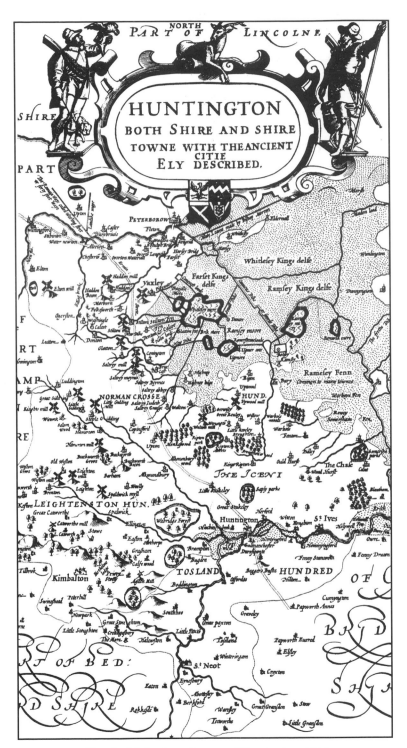

Detail of John Speed's map of Huntingdon, 1610.

THE DARWEN COUNTY HISTORY SERIES

A History of
HUNTINGDONSHIRE

Michael Wickes

Phillimore

1995

Published by
PHILIMORE & CO. LTD.
Shopwyke Manor Barn, Chichester, West Sussex

First published 1985
Revised edition 1995

© Michael Wickes, 1995

ISBN 0 85033 953 7

Printed and bound in Great Britain by
BUTLER & TANNER LTD.
Frome, Somerset

To my wife Rosie

Contents

List of Illustrations 9
Acknowledgements 11
Foreword by the Rt Hon John Major, MP, Prime Minister 13
Introduction 15

 1 Prehistoric Huntingdonshire 17
 2 Roman Huntingdonshire 22
 3 Anglo-Saxon Huntingdonshire 30
 4 Medieval Huntingdonshire: The Years of Expansion 38
 5 Medieval Huntingdonshire: The Years of Decline 48
 6 The Medieval Monasteries 53
 7 The Tudor Era 62
 8 Oliver Cromwell and the English Civil War 70
 9 Agriculture and the Rural Community (1540-1750) 76
10 Towns and Trade 87
11 The County Community of Gentry 97
12 Religious Dissent 107
13 Huntingdonshire Schools 113
14 Agriculture in the 19th Century 117
15 Railways, Reforms and Redcoats 125
16 The 20th Century 130

Select Bibliography 137
Index 141

List of Illustrations

1. Bronze-Age cinerary urn found at Brampton 18
2. Map of Prehistoric Huntingdonshire 19
3. Bronze-Age spear heads found at Conington and Ramsey 20
4. Bronze-Age axe heads found at Wood Walton and Great Raveley 20
5. Ermine Street 21
6. Map of Roman Huntingdonshire 23
7. Roman stone coffins 24
8. Roman pottery cup made in the Nene valley 25
9. Roman carved stone column found near Castor 26
10. Roman Christian church silver from *Durobrivae* 27
11. Roman silver cup 28
12. Anglo-Saxon bronze brooch found at St Ives 31
13. Church at Great Paxton 33
14. Anglo-Saxon arches in church at Great Paxton 34
15. Anglo-Saxon coin minted at Huntingdon 35
16. Anglo-Saxon coin minted at Huntingdon 35
17. Abbot's Chair 36
18. Hundred stone at Leighton Bromswold 36
19. Map showing Huntingdonshire in 1086 39
20. Spur, sword, sword hilt and arrow-head 41
21. St Mary's church, Bluntisham 43
22. Church at Steeple Gidding 44
23. Map of medieval markets in Huntingdonshire 45
24. Church at Great Staughton 46
25. Memorial brass of Sir William Moyne and his wife 49
26. Memorial brass to man and wife, *c.*1400 49
27. Map showing the places of origin of Huntingdon taxpayers in 1332 50
28. Conington church 51
29. Holy Cross church, Bury 52
30. Medieval bridge and chapel over the Ouse, St Ives 53
31. 15th-century chapel on bridge over the Ouse, St Ives 54
32. Gatehouse at Ramsey Abbey 55
33. Gatehouse at Ramsey Abbey, from the inside 56
34. School on the site of Ramsey Abbey 57
35. Bishop's Palace at Buckden 59
36. Early brickwork at the Bishop's Palace 61
37. Map of monastic lands in Huntingdonshire, 1530 63
38. Memorial brass to William Taylard 64
39. Memorial brass to William Halles 65
40. Leighton Bromswold church, interior 66

41. Little Gidding church 67
42. Cover page of Puritan pamphlet 68
43. Memorial brass to John Ferrar 69
44. *Haycock Inn* at Wansford 69
45. Cavalry sword from the Civil War period 70
46. Halberd found at St Ives 71
47. Bust of Oliver Cromwell 72
48. Statue of Oliver Cromwell, St Ives 72
49. Map of Huntingdonshire in the Civil War 73
50. Plan of the Parliamentarian fort at Horsey Hill 74
51. Winter landscape near Wood Walton 78
52. Summer landscape near Wood Walton 79
53. House at Wistow, dated 1662 80
54. Brick and thatch at Offord Darcy 81
55. Thatched house at Wistow 82
56. Cottages at Easton 83
57. Detail of John Speed's map of Huntingdon, 1610 88
58. Title page of the *St Ives Mercury*, 1719 89
59. Coaching inn at Buckden 91
60. Bridge over the Nene, Wansford 92
61. Market-place at St Neots 93
62. Barges on the Ouse at St Ives 94
63. St Mary's church, St Neots 96
64. Kimbolton Castle, *c*.1933-34 97
65. Hinchingbrooke House 98
66. Aerial view of Hinchingbrooke House 99
67. Map showing major estates in Huntingdonshire, 1750 100
68. Church at Little Gidding 102
69. Manor house at Hilton 103
70. Wooden tower on church at Hail Weston 104
71. Village green and earth maze at Hilton 106
72. 18th-century Baptist chapel at Great Gidding 108
73. Nonconformist church at St Neots 110
74. Methodist chapel at Huntingdon 110
75. Map showing the Ecclesiastical Census of 1851 111
76. Former grammar school, Huntingdon 114
77. Kimbolton Castle 116
78. Map showing Huntingdonshire parishes, *c*.1811 118
79. Old bridge and 19th-century mill, Huntingdon 119
80. 19th-century mill on the Ouse 121
81. Blacksmith's gravestone, Houghton 122
82. Water pump, St Ives 123
83. Huntingdon railway bridge 125
84. Map showing the railways of Huntingdonshire 126
85. Steam trains near Buckden 127
86. Map showing local government districts 128
87. Model of ship made from animal bones 129
88. Carrier's van at Glatton 131
89. Harvest scene, *c*.1910 132
90. Chinese bridge at Godmanchester 133
91. Pill-box near Ramsey 134
92. John Major, MP, with constituents 136

Colour Plates

facing page

I	The *Bell Inn* at Stilton	32
II	Hinchingbrooke House near Huntingdon	32
III	Kimbolton Castle	33
IV	Almshouses and church at Ramsey	33
V	St Ives from the by-pass	64
VI	Jubilee Clock Tower at Warboys	64
VII	Abbots Ripton church	65
VIII	Clock tower at Fenstanton	96
IX	Chincsc bridgc at Godmanchester	96
X	River Ouse at Hemingford Grey	97
XI	Houghton Mill	128
XII	Portrait of Oliver Cromwell	128
XIII	Ramsey Drain near Ramsey St Mary's	129
XIV	Barograph at Bluntisham	129

Acknowledgements

I wish to thank everyone who helped me with the preparation of the second edition of *A History of Huntingdonshire*. I owe a great debt of gratitude to Bob Burn-Murdoch, curator of the Norris Museum in St Ives, because of his provision of museum artifacts for photographs and sketches. Philip Saunders, deputy County Archivist at the Huntingdon Record Office, was also very helpful. I would also like to thank Faber and Faber Ltd., with the Eliot estate, for their permission to reproduce extracts from *The Four Quartets* by T.S. Eliot. I must also acknowledge the kind assistance given by the Rt Hon John Major, MP for Huntingdon, in his contribution of a foreword for this second edition.

Above all, I would like to thank Bill Wright, an artist from Appledore in North Devon, who drew the illustrations for this edition. Robert Whytehead and Michael Nix have also kindly allowed me to re-use the photographs and maps that appeared in the first edition. Finally, I give my thanks to anyone in the Huntingdon area who assisted me in any way, especially thinking of James and Christine Edwards who once again gave me hospitality.

MICHAEL J.L. WICKES, MA
January 1995

HOUSE OF COMMONS
LONDON SW1A 0AA

Huntingdonshire has a long and proud tradition, a county of attractive villages, historic buildings, evocative landscapes and relaxing waterways.

But with the extensive development that has taken place over the past twenty years, Huntingdonshire is also very well placed to move forward into the 21st century, particularly with the completion of the A1/M1 link which has given us unrivalled access, not only to the rest of the country but also to the rest of Europe.

When Norma and I first came to Huntingdonshire on a cold November evening in 1976, little did we know what an important part the area was to play in our lives. We have lived here for over 16 years; our children have grown up here, they went to local schools, our son played football for local teams and our daughter still plays in local orchestras.

It is our home and a most welcome place to which to return each weekend, after the noise and activity of Downing Street. I like Huntingdonshire, I like the people, I like its landscapes. I know that after reading Michael Wickes' excellent history of this fascinating part of East Anglia, you will like it too.

THE RT HON JOHN MAJOR, MP
Prime Minister

Introduction

I first visited Huntingdonshire during the winter of 1974, and made my home there for most of the next seven years. I am, therefore, not a native of Huntingdonshire but someone who came to love the rural regions of this county, particularly the upland claylands around the Giddings. My interest in the history of Huntingdonshire became very strong, and this book is partly the product of several short studies made between 1976 and 1981. I moved to north Devon in May 1981, where I now make a living as a freelance genealogist, but I still retain a strong affection for Huntingdonshire.

A history of the former county is certainly long overdue, since the last book that concentrated exclusively upon Huntingdonshire was the *Victoria County History*, published in 1926. Sadly, the old county was abolished in 1974, and the parishes within it were merged into greater Cambridgeshire. However, it is good to know that the Huntingdon District Council made a decision during 1984 to change their title to the Huntingdonshire District Council, thus helping to keep alive the memory of the former county.

It is difficult to remain detached when writing a book like this, and one is bound to be more interested in certain parts of the county or in specific periods of its history. It is not always possible to align with T.S. Eliot when he was writing about the Civil War era:

> We cannot revive old factions,
> We cannot restore old policies
> Or follow an antique drum.
> These men, and those who opposed them,
> And those whom they opposed
> Accept the constitution of silence
> And are folded in a single party.

(Little Gidding: T.S. Eliot)

I therefore apologise in advance for any bias that may have influenced my historical deductions, and I also hope that future readers of this book will come to value this small area of England that once was known as Huntingdonshire.

MICHAEL J.L. WICKES, MA
1994

1

Prehistoric Huntingdonshire

The Ouse Valley

The county of Huntingdonshire is located in the east Midlands of England, between the Fenland to the east, the river Nene to the north and the valley of the Ouse to the south. The county was a territory of Anglo-Saxon or Danish origin, so its boundaries would have had no significance to primitive man or to the later Roman colonisers. It is more realistic to talk about Huntingdonshire at this date as a group of four geographical regions: the valleys of the rivers Nene and Ouse, the area of peat Fenland to the east, and the upland clay soils of the central and western areas.

The Ouse valley was the area of greatest significance for the later county, being the location of the county town of Huntingdon and the three small market towns of St Ives, Godmanchester and St Neots. The soil is a light and fertile alluvial gravel, ideal for the earliest forms of agriculture which were developed during the Neolithic era (3000 to 1800 B.C.). However, there is evidence that the pre-agricultural peoples of the Old Stone Age (40000 to 3000 B.C.) also roamed through the valley. The Palaeolithic and Mesolithic peoples of this period formed mobile groups of hunters and food-gatherers, leaving few remains behind them except for their flint tools and weapons. Occasional finds of flints from this period have been recorded throughout the valley. A flint-working site has been discovered at St Neots, and a camp floor dating to *c.*6000 B.C. at Hemingford Abbots.

The Neolithic people with their primitive form of agriculture, their use of pottery, and their new techniques of flint-working must have appeared in the Ouse valley soon after 3000 B.C. The first significant change in the local landscape occurred during this period, as the woodland in the valley was cleared, providing both land for the growing of grain crops and pasture for cattle, pigs and sheep. The discovery of pottery sherds indicates the presence of Neolithic man at St Ives, Fenstanton, Buckden and, just across the county border, at Eaton Socon. However, the only positive proof for the existence of settlements in the valley comes from Little Paxton, where a 'D-shaped' Neolithic hut was excavated in 1967.

The use of metal first occurred in the Ouse valley after 2000 B.C., when the 'Beaker culture' appeared in England. It should be emphasised, however, that bronze weapons and tools remained relatively rare until later in this period,

1 Bronze-Age cinerary urn found at Brampton, now in the Norris Museum at St Ives.

and the use of flints was still very common. One characteristic of this bronze-working people was their funeral customs: round barrows and burials containing beaker pottery. Most round barrows in Huntingdonshire probably disappeared under the plough long ago, since they were mainly raised on the valley floors of the Nene and Ouse. Ring-ditches that appear on aerial photographs are often the remnants of Bronze-Age round barrows. In 1966 five such ring-ditches were excavated at Brampton, and the archaeologists enthusiastically noted in their report that the site showed 'startling proof that Huntingdonshire and the Ouse valley is no mere Bronze-Age backwater, but may well be closely connected with the first waves of Beaker settlement in Britain'. A large cinerary urn from a Brampton barrow-site can now be seen in the Norris Museurn in St Ives. A similar ring-ditch site has been found at Rectory Farm, one mile north-east of Godmanchester, while beaker burials have come from Brampton, Houghton, and the Offords. The beaker found at Houghton is also in the Norris Museum.

Iron was first used in Huntingdonshire after 650 B.C., and an expanding population led to the intensification of agriculture in the Ouse valley. Settlements became firmly established, as indicated by crop-marks showing the outlines of small fields, stockyards and drove roads which appear on aerial photographs. Iron-Age farms have been found at Godmanchester, Little Paxton, Buckden, Brampton and St Ives.

The Nene Valley

The Nene valley on the northern border of Huntingdonshire was more attractive to primitive settlers than the Ouse valley to the south. However, only the southern bank of the river Nene can appear in this county study due to the later use of the river as the county boundary: this reduces the value of the map on page 19 as a guide to the overall importance of the Nene valley during this period. The most outstanding prehistoric site in the valley, for instance, is at Fengate, just over the county border east of Peterborough. Occupation was continuous here from the appearance of a single Neolithic farm (*c*.3000 B.C.) until the emergence of an Iron-Age village of considerable size. The soils on the south bank of the Nene are alluvial gravels and limestone, again very suitable for primitive agriculture. However, Neolithic farmers left few remains on the south bank except for a wooden henge at Elton, a site that was undoubtedly of minor importance in comparison with the great religious complex at Maxey again north of the county boundary.

There was a general population increase and an intensification of agriculture in the Nene valley during the Iron Age, even more extreme than the population expansion that occurred in the Ouse valley. One Iron-Age farmstead that was occupied well into the Roman period has been found south of Orton Longueville, while aerial photography south of Orton Waterville has revealed the stockyards and fields of another farm. At least eighteen similar settlements have been identified on the Huntingdonshire bank of the river Nene, 11 of which were occupied into the Roman period.

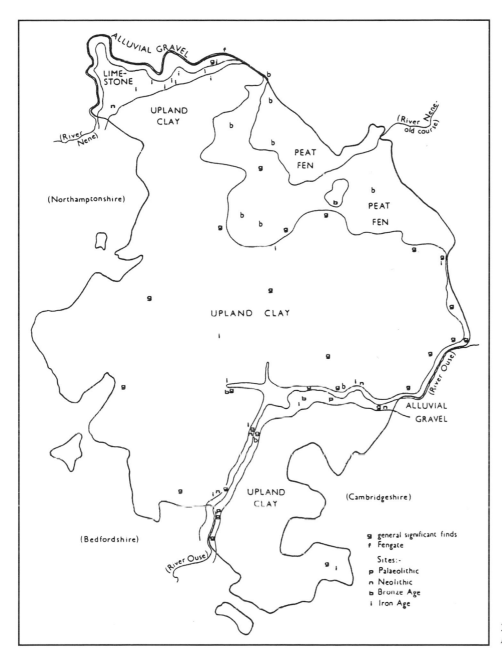

2 *Map of Prehistoric Huntingdonshire.*

The Fenland

The area of Fenland in north-east Huntingdonshire is composed of a rich peat soil, formed by partially undecayed fen vegetation being deposited in the fresh-water marshes which covered this area until the 17th century. However, this part of the county was not always peat fen, as it formed dry land during the Old Stone Age, accessible to roaming bands of Palaeolithic and Mesolithic hunters.

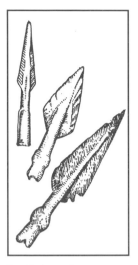

3 *Bronze-Age spear heads found at Conington and Ramsey, now in the Norris Museum at St Ives.*

A tall forest covered the fens during late Mesolithic and Neolithic times, which was partially cleared by Neolithic peoples. The rising of the sea level (*c.*2500 B.C.) led to the death of this forest, the trees of which are still sometimes recovered from the modern fens as 'bog-oaks'. The Fenland basin became a vast lagoon between 2500 and 2000 B.C., but then the landscape reverted to a dry state during the Bronze Age. It suffered its final freshwater inundation after 500 B.C., and the marshes were avoided as settlement sites by Iron-Age man, so increasing population pressures in the Nene and Ouse valleys.

The accessibility of the Fenland during the Bronze Age means that finds from this period are common all over the peat fen in north-east Huntingdonshire. Discoveries include a Bronze-Age settlement and barrow-field near Ramsey, two bronze spearheads from Conington Fen, a bronze socketed axe in Yaxley Fen, and at least three wooden dug-out canoes. One of these boats was found near Stanground in 1828, another at Whittlesey Mere, and the third at Warboys Fen in 1909. The last example was 37 feet long, and its flat bottom was three inches thick.

Iron-Age settlements in the fens were sited around the edge of the marshes. One such settlement has been discovered at Somersham, whilst another was located near Wood Walton. The sites of these villages enabled their inhabitants to take advantage of both the summer pastures in the fens (when the winter floods receded) and the woods on the upland clayland to west and south of the settlements. One significant Iron-Age discovery from this area was the chariot lynch-pins found near Somersham, now on display in the Norris Museum, St Ives.

The Upland Clayland

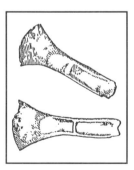

4 *Bronze-Age axe heads found at Wood Walton and Great Raveley, now in the Norris Museum at St Ives.*

The upland clay soils in western Huntingdonshire have always been seen as marginal land for agriculture, due to their poor drainage and intractable nature. There is no evidence that prehistoric man settled in this area in anything like the numbers of those who lived in the fens or the river valleys. Occasional flint implements have been found in a uniform pattern over the upland clays, but they were either left by nomadic hunters of the Palaeolithic or Mesolithic periods, or by settlers or woodcutters who lived in isolated forest clearings during Iron-Age or Roman times. Flint tools like these are generally marked on the map with a 'g' symbol. No other finds have appeared in these areas that date from the Neolithic or Bronze-Age periods.

After 650 B.C., it is likely that the pressure of population in the river valleys led to some penetration of the mixed deciduous forests that covered the upland clay soils. Few prehistoric trackways crossing the clayland have been found, although the 'Bullock Road' later used as a drovers' way possibly originated as a prehistoric track. It certainly followed the line of the ridge skirting the Fenland, but only Roman remains have been found along its route. There was possibly another prehistoric trackway under the Roman road from Alconbury to Leicester, perhaps a means of access between the Fenland and the Nene valley in Northamptonshire. At least five Iron-Age pottery vessels have been unearthed near Salome Lodge on the line of the later Roman road, possibly indicating an Iron-Age settlement situated near the prehistoric trackway. Certainly, a single Iron-Age farm has been located at Alconbury Hill at the southern end of the Bullock Road. Isolated Iron-Age finds sites have also come from other clayland sites, including an uninscribed coin from Great Gransden, and a beaker from Dean, near Kimbolton.

5 *Ermine Street, south of Huntingdon.*

2

Roman Huntingdonshire

The Roman Conquest

British reached the final stage of its development as a primitive Iron-Age culture during the lifetime of Christ. Its native population had started to use iron tools and weapons, but they still lived at the mercy of poor communications, inefficient forms of agriculture, and the bellicose dispositions of tribal chieftains. This picture changed dramatically between the years A.D. 43 to 47 when Britain endured a military conquest by a distant Mediterranean civilisation. The impact of the succeeding four centuries of Roman rule changed the face of Celtic Britain beyond recognition, and clearly left its mark on the later county of Huntingdonshire, as the map on page 23 indicates. Roman roads later traversed the upland clays in all directions, whilst two thriving towns in the Nene and Ouse valleys became agricultural and industrial centres of some importance.

The local Celtic tribes did not accept this new domination without protest. The Catuvellauni was the dominant tribe in most of Huntingdonshire just before the conquest, probably sharing a border on the Nene with the Coritani. There was also an unclear boundary in the fens with the Iceni. The Romans constructed a military road northwards from Sandy in Bedfordshire to run east of the Ouse valley to the present site of Godmanchester, where a fort was built. Then they marched northwards along the fen edge and constructed a second fort at Water Newton in the Nene valley. A third and larger fortress was built at Longthorpe on the northern bank of the Nene. This site dates to A.D. 50-60, and was probably used as an outpost against the Iceni in the east. However, the Roman presence in the area had barely been established before the Iceni rose in revolt between A.D. 60-61. About two thousand soldiers from the Longthorpe fortress were sent south to contain Queen Boudicca and her tribesmen, but they were defeated. This resulted in the sacking of several new towns throughout East Anglia, including the small civilian settlement that had appeared at Godmanchester. A layer of burnt building debris dating from this period has been excavated. Roman control of the Huntingdonshire area, therefore, was not consolidated until after the defeat of the Iceni in A.D. 61.

The Ouse Valley

The Roman presence in the Ouse valley between A.D. 61 and the fifth century was never as decisive as it was in the Nene valley. The main outpost of Roman

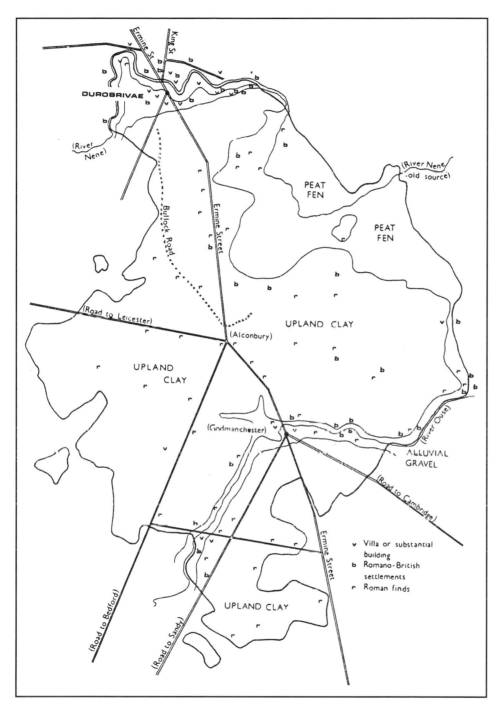

6 *Map of Roman Huntingdonshire.*

civilisation in the valley was the town of Godmanchester, which was rebuilt on a planned basis enclosing 20 acres after its destruction by the Iceni. The fort at Godmanchester was only used during the early years of the invasion, but the

7 *Roman stone coffins dating to the third or fourth centuries, found near Water Newton, now at the Norris Museum at St Ives.*

civilian settlement at its gates expanded to support a population not far short of three thousand people during the third century. A *mansio* or inn to accommodate imperial couriers was built in the western sector of the town soon after A.D. 120, together with a large bath-house containing a series of cold and hot baths. A *basilica* or town hall was built during the third century, probably to mark Godmanchester's achievement of self-government as a *vicus*. Town walls were also constructed during the third century, although archaeological evidence suggests that part of the western section was left uncompleted.

Most of the town's population lived in humble round huts, soon to be superseded by two-bay rectangular buildings. The local people were dependent upon agriculture for their livelihood, besides benefiting from Godmanchester's function as a market town. It is believed by some local historians that the rural territory farmed by the Roman townspeople later became the ecclesiastical parish of Godmancheter. About 267 acres of this land probably formed the intensively cultivated 'infield', judging from the scatter of Roman pottery lying over it which was probably carried out from the town in the rubbish. Another 711 acres apparently formed the 'outfield', land lying on the parish boundaries that was cropped for three or four years, before being allowed to lie fallow for about five years. There were also two villas in the immediate vicinity of Godmanchester, one on Mill Common on the north bank of the Ouse (near the site of Huntingdon) and the other at Rectory Farm to the north-east of the town.

A series of Roman roads soon radiated out from Godmanchester in all directions. The most important was Ermine Street, running between London and York. It was certainly a later feature than the fort at Godmanchester, since excavations have shown it ran over the top of the fort. It was probably constructed soon after the latter was abandoned in the mid-first century. The bridge that carried it over the Ouse was built in the early second century; before then it crossed the river by a ford further upstream. The stone piers of a bridge to carry it across the Nene (near the town of *Durobrivae*) have also been located. Another road that converged upon Godmanchester was the *Via Devena* from Cambridge. The military road from Sandy in Bedfordshire was replaced by a new road at the end of the Roman period.

None of these roads took a route along the valley of the Ouse, one more piece of evidence pointing to the densely populated state of the valley at this time. It would not have been in the interests of the Romans to alienate the local natives by building roads through valuable farmland when they could construct them over the largely unfarmed areas of upland clay

Most of the farmland on the banks of the Ouse was worked by groups of Romano-British people living in settlements scattered along the valley floor. Romano-British farmsteads have been located at Stirtloe near Buckden, the Brickhills estate near Eyncsbury, Holywell, Houghton Hill, Little Paxton, Eaton Ford near St Neots and Monks Hardwick, north-east of St Neots. These Romano-British farmsteads generally produced both livestock products and grain crops. The cereals were probably grown for home consumption while some of the animal products were supplied to the Roman army based in the north of Britain. The Ouse was used as the principal means of transporting bulk goods. Ballast and other objects found in the river at St Ives probably came from a Roman barge. Products from the Ouse valley farms were taken downstream to Earith, whence they were sent northwards along the Car Dyke, the Roman drainage canal that cut a course across the Fens towards Lincoln.

Several small industries existed in the Ouse valley which gave employment to a few of its Romano-British inhabitants. A pottery kiln has been found on the north edge of Godmanchester that dates to the mid-third century. A potters' quarter, containing at least four kilns and dating to the third or fourth centuries, was situated at the Romano-British settlement near Earith. At least one workshop located at Godmanchester was used for making bronze and iron objects: this can be dated to the early second century.

Objects found in the Ouse valley indicate the presence of a multi-religious society in this area during the Roman period. Three successive temples have been excavated at Godmanchester, near the *mansio* and bath-house. They were apparently dedicated to a local Celtic god, judging from the discovery of a group of bronze votive plaques at the site. Unknown elsewhere, this god was possibly the local deity of the Ouse. The occasional discovery of statuettes demonstrates that other religions were practised in the valley. Two Venus pipeclay figurines have come from Godmanchester; a bronze statuette of Mars Ultor was found at Bury Fen near Bluntisham; and a bronze statuette of Mercury from Model Farm near Fenstanton. The discovery of a late third-century collection of church silver at

8 *Roman pottery cup made in the Nene valley, dating to the third century A.D., now in the Peterborough Museum.*

Water Newton in the Nene valley indicates that there was a Christian church at *Durobrivae* by this date. Nothing comparable has yet been found in the Ouse valley, although a fourth-century lead tank has been dredged from the Ouse near Godmanchester. It is similar to others found elsewhere, which were decorated with the Christian *Chi-Rho* monogram. It seems unlikely that they were used as fonts as they are sometimes found in pairs, but they may be connected with ritual ablutions. The later Christian church at Godmanchester (St Mary's) stands in the centre of several Roman cemeteries outside the former town walls, indicating that it may cover the site of an earlier Roman Christian church.

The Nene Valley

The Roman colonisation of the Nene valley was even more impressive than their presence in the Ouse valley. Their earliest appearance was again military. The five-acre fort at Water Newton was built in the mid-first century, to guard the crossing of the Nene, while a larger 30-acre fortress was built on the north bank of the Nene at Longthorpe. However, the training ground for the troops at Longthorpe was apparently on the south bank (now the grounds of Nene Park).

A civilian settlement soon appeared at the gates of the Water Newton fort. The later parish boundary now separates the town of *Durobrivae* from the Water Newton fort; and the parish that contains the site of *Durobrivae* is called Chesterton (meaning the 'town' near the 'chester' or Roman town). The name *Durobrivae* comes from the Latin *duro* meaning 'walled place' and from the Celtic *briva* meaning 'bridge'. The name was probably transferred from the Water Newton fort as the town walls were built late in the Roman period. The line of the Durobrivae walls can still be seen today as earthworks, containing about forty-four acres, but the suburbs eventually expanded in size to six or seven times that extent. The interior area of the town has not yet been excavated, but aerial photographs have revealed the outline of at least one large building, possibly a *mansio* similar to that found at Godmanchester. *Durobrivae* was originally known as a *vicus*, but it may have become a *civitas* or regional capital by the fourth century. Some authorities believe that it became the regional capital for the fens. However, its territory as a *vicus* was still considerable. Boundary stones have been found at Sawtry and Thrapston that apparently relate to the borders of the *vicus* of *Durobrivae*. It seems plausible that the two *vicus* territories of *Durobrivae* and Godmanchester met on a line running from east to west near Sawtry, thus dividing the later county of Huntingdonshire into two halves.

A town of the size of Durobrivae drew upon the agricultural resources of a considerable area in order to maintain its population. There were several Roman villas in the Nene valley supplying some of this produce, positioned about one and half miles from each other. These villa estates presumably consisted of meadowland on the valley floor, arable land on higher ground, and had access to woodland on the upland slopes to the south.

The local industry which enabled *Durobrivae* to expand to its great size was the production of pottery. The Nene valley is the area of Roman Britain associated with the style known as 'castorware', which first appeared about

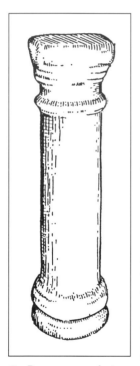

9 *Roman carved stone column found near Castor in the Nene valley, now in the Peterborough Museum.*

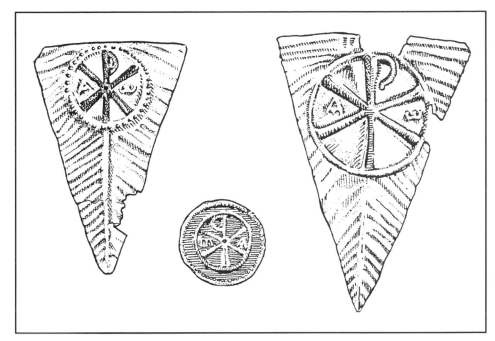

10 *Roman Christian church silver from* Durobrivae *(near Water Newton) dating to the late third or fourth centuries A.D., now in the British Museum, London.*

125 A.D. This industry reached its peak during the fourth century and its products were exported to all corners of Roman Britain. The manufacture of pottery was forbidden inside the town, so the kilns were located either in the suburbs or along the banks of the Nene as far west as Stibbington and as far east as Stanground. The river itself was used for the transport of raw materials and the finished products. Pots supplied to the army in the north were taken downstream by barge to join the Car Dyke just east of modern Peterborough. Fine examples of castorware pots can be seen in the Peterborough Museum, including one specimen found near Water Newton depicting two gladiators in combat.

There were many other thriving industries in the Nene valley. A local school of mosaicists was based at *Durobrivae*, which made mosaic floors for local villas and indeed for others throughout the east Midlands. There was also iron working in the valley: one such industrial site, complete with furnaces and pits, has been found at Orton Longueville. Stone quarries were excavated at Sibson in 1959, and three unfinished or rejected statues were discovered. Salt extraction was another local industry as the Nene was still tidal at this date. One probable 'saltern' site has been found near Stanground.

Numerous finds in the Nene valley attest to the great prosperity of the region during the later Roman period. The two most famous discoveries are the mid-fourth-century hoard of gold coins, and the late third-century hoard of church silver, both found within the walls of *Durobrivae*. The first find consisted of two pieces of folded silver plate, and 30 gold coins dated between 330 and 350 A.D. The hoard of church silver is the earliest collection of Christian church plate found anywhere in the Roman empire (other early hoards date to the sixth century), and it demonstrates that Christianity had taken hold in an

11 *Silver cup found in hoard of Roman Christian silver from* Durobrivae *(near Water Newton), dating to late third or fourth centuries A.D., now in the British Museum, London.*

outlying Roman province before it was officially recognised by the Imperial government. The silver objects were hidden in the ground during a time of persecution during the early fourth century. One of the inscriptions on the objects refers to an *altare* or sacred place: perhaps an early Christian church was located somewhere in the town. Both these hoards are now on display in the British Museum.

The Fenland

Much research has been devoted during recent years to the study of the Roman colonisation of the Fenland. The partial drainage and occupation of the fens had reached its zenith by the late second century, suffered a reversal during the third century and was then resumed during the fourth century. Much of this colonisation of the marshes occurred on the silt lands near the Wash, while the peat fen in the south, of which north-east Huntingdonshire was a part, remained more sparsely inhabited. The marshland east of Sawtry was especially low-lying and boggy, so Romano-British settlements in this area were confined to the fen edge, at Earith, Colne, Somersham, Farcet, Sawtry, Yaxley and Stocking Close, near Monk's Wood.

These Romano-British farmers were mainly engaged in livestock farming in order to produce meat, leather and dairy products (pottery cheese presses have been discovered on many sites). Finds of animal bones suggest that wool and dairy farming was more common than meat production. Villas were generally non-existent on the northern silt fens, but they are occasionally found on the fen edge around the southern peat fens. One example in Huntingdonshire is at Somersham, where a substantial building made with Barnack stone from the Nene valley was found on Turkington Hill. Some authorities believe that much of the Fenland was drained and owned by one organising power: the Roman emperors. However, this imperial state probably did not extend into the southern peat fens, due to the obstacle of native landownership, which was not present in the north. The land in the peat fens of Huntingdonshire was probably owned or tenanted by Romano-British farmers who paid their rents to individual villa owners.

An area of intense Romano-British occupation has been discovered along the fen edge near Somersham, Colne and Earith, where five or six settlements have so far been found. It is interesting in this respect that 'Colne' is a Celtic name derived from a local waterway. The dedication of Colne church is to St Helen, the mother of the Emperor Constantine who lived during the third and fourth centuries. It is possible that this church (which fell down in 1896) stood on the site of an early Roman Christian church, and that a settlement of British Christians continued to live in the area during the early Anglo-Saxon period.

The Upland Clayland

The map of Roman Huntingdonshire illustrates that farmers of this period were penetrating the forests that still covered much of the upland areas of the county. However, the evidence for permanent settlements is still very scanty. A substantial building, possibly a villa, was excavated at Rushey Farm near Great Staughton in 1958, and mosaic floors were discovered. Romano-British settlements have been identified at Wyton, Wistow, Woodhurst, and Broughton, on the upland area that forms a peninsula between the Fens and the Ouse valley. Much of this region was probably cleared for farming by Romano-British settlers, which is interesting in view of its later association with woodland. Place-names such as Upwood, Wood Walton, Woodhurst and Oldhurst suggest the presence of an extensive forest, as does the name for the Anglo-Saxon hundred which covered this area of Huntingdonshire (Hurstingstone comes from the word 'Hurstingas', meaning 'forest dwellers'). The area probably reverted to forest during the early Anglo-Saxon era.

Roman finds in other parts of the upland clayland are associated with the roads that crossed these areas. Roman objects have been discovered along the line of Ermine Street, including a Romano-British burial mound near Great Stukeley and another barrow of probable Romano-British origin just south of Chesterton. The road from Alconbury to Leicester passed a Romano-British settlement at Salome Wood, where several objects have been found, including late-third century pottery and human bones. The road from Alconbury to Bedford, a section of which was excavated near Grafham Water during the early 1960s, passed near to the villa site at Great Staughton, and another possible settlement site at Thorpe Lodge Farm near Ellington. Roman finds can also be associated with the Bullock Road. Pottery and a hoard of third-century coins have come from Hill Top Farm near Coppingford while coins and pottery have been found at Cold Harbour Farm near Steeple Gidding. The original function of the Bullock Road remains obscure, but it may have been used as a drove road during the Roman period. Herds of livestock would thus be kept off Ermine Street, which was reserved for military traffic and civilian vehicles.

Alconbury was a meeting-point for this network of Roman roads, and it is possible that a sizeable Roman settlement remains to be discovered here. Several Roman objects have been found in the parish, including coins and metal objects from Alconbury Hill and pottery near Ermine Street. Skeletons, and a coin dated around 300 A.D., were found in the garden of the manor house in 1913.

No real evidence for the presence of early Christianity exists on the upland clayland, except for a mysterious woodcarving that can be seen in the church chancel at Great Gidding. This carving, inscribed with the date 1614, recites the Latin palindrome 'Rotas opera tenet Arepo sator'. The palindrome was possibly used by early Christians as a secret sign, as the letters can be arranged to form the word 'paternoster' twice, making a cross. Examples of this word puzzle have been found on the wall of a Roman house at Cirencester in Gloucestershire and on a piece of pottery found during the excavation of the Roman fort at Manchester. However, it will probably never be known why this palindrome was carved onto a wooden tablet in the 17th century. Could the craftsman have found a Roman inscription and copied it? The Great Gidding tablet is thus possibly one more clue indicating the presence of Christianity in Huntingdonshire at least three centuries before St Augustine landed in Kent to convert the Saxons in A.D. 597.

3

Anglo-Saxon Huntingdonshire

The Anglo-Saxon Conquest

The Anglo-Saxon conquest of Roman Britain which took place during the fifth century can be seen as a pagan interlude between an era of Roman Christian civilization and the birth of a young and fervent Anglo-Saxon Christianity in the seventh century. In Huntingdonshire, the pagan invaders first occupied the prime agricultural land in the river valleys, where their cemeteries, rich in grave goods, have generally been found. Evidence from these cemeteries and other archaeological sites has shown that the Anglo-Saxons arrived in the Nene and Ouse valleys at an early date. The official end of Roman Britain is placed in the year A.D. 410, when the last Roman troops and officials were withdrawn. However, the first Anglo-Saxons in Huntingdonshire had appeared by A.D. 400, and stable communities had emerged in the river valleys during the early fifth century. These pagan Anglo-Saxons probably came as mercenaries, hired by Roman officials and town governments. Early Anglo-Saxon pottery associated with late Roman sherds has been found in Godmanchester, despite a lack of pagan cemeteries in the vicinity. The town had been sacked during the late third century, possibly by sea-going marauders, and the hiring of Anglo-Saxon mercenaries was probably one consequence of this.

The current view held by historians is that Roman Britain did not disappear overnight in a holocaust of fire and bloodshed. There is a growing body of evidence which shows that the Anglo-Saxons participated in a more prolonged and peaceful annexation of the rural areas, so permitting the survival of some Romano-British settlements. This appears to be true in the case of Huntingdonshire. Pagan Anglo-Saxon remains have been found in association with a late Romano-British farm at Orton Longueville in the Nene valley, while place-names such as Colne, Nene and Ouse are Celtic in origin. The survival of Celtic river-names is especially significant since the incoming Anglo-Saxons would have adopted the old names for features that were known to large numbers of people, only introducing new names for their own settlements.

The more elaborate Roman structures soon collapsed after the Anglo-Saxon conquest. The large pottery industry located near *Durobrivae* disappeared shortly after it had reached its peak of production during the fourth century. This is the main reason why *Durobrivae*, with an economy dependent upon a national market, is now an abandoned site in a grass field, while Godmanchester, with a local agricultural economy, survived as a small market town. The elaborate drainage system in the fens also collapsed upon the disappearance of Roman influence, leading to the partial abandonment of the Fenland during most of the Anglo-Saxon era.

Some Romano-British farmers almost certainly survived in Huntingdonshire as the Anglo-Saxon population expanded. These people generally inhabited the more remote areas, notably the Fenland marshes and the upland woods. St Guthlac of Crowland Abbey referred to Fenland people still speaking Celtic during the eighth century, whilst a monastic official at Ely in the seventh century was called by the British name of Owen. An inscription with a prayer for Owen's soul can still be seen on a memorial cross in Ely Cathedral.

The first Anglo-Saxon colonisation

Documents such as the 'Tribal Hidage', which dates to the seventh century, indicate that Huntingdonshire was inhabited by two or more small Anglo-Saxon tribes before the eighth century. These petty kingdoms were eventually conquered by the rising power of Mercia to the west. The tribe that occupied the Nene valley near the site of Peterborough was apparently called the 'Gwyras', according to the writings of the historian Bede, and to a charter of 957. Another tribe called the 'Hyrstingas', meaning forest-dwellers, lived around the Ouse valley and on the wooded uplands: they are commemorated in the hundred-name of Hurstingstone. Other tribes that may have occupied small areas of the county were the 'Sweordora' and the 'Spalda', the latter being suggested by the village-name of Spaldwick.

12 *Anglo-Saxon bronze brooch found at St Ives, dated c.600 A.D., now in Norris Museum at St Ives.*

The influence of the early Anglo-Saxon church in the formation of the county of Huntingdonshire should not be under-estimated. A monastery was established at Peterborough (then called Medehamstede) during the mid-seventh century, and monks from this foundation were probably responsible for the conversion of the Nene valley and beyond. Monks from the monastery founded at Ely in 673 were probably occupied with missionary work in the southern half of Huntingdonshire, as is suggested by the later appearance of Ely Abbey estates at Somersham and Spaldwick. Descendants of Romano-British Christians were probably also active in this work. The first husband of St Etheldreda, the foundress of Ely Abbey, was a Christian named Tonbert, a 'prince of the Fenmen'.

The pattern of rural settlements in Huntingdonshire which we recognise today was established before the Danish conquest in the ninth century. Most modern village names were recorded in Domesday Book, written in 1086, and the chart (overleaf) demonstrates that just over half of these village names appeared in Anglo-Saxon land charters dating between 650 and 1055. However this chart should not be used to date the first appearance of an individual settlement. Many village names which belonged to primary settlements were first recorded in Domesday Book, while several names that first appeared in early charters were daughter villages of the primary settlements. Most villages recorded on land charters were situated on estates held by monastic institutions, which were more inclined to record their holdings on documents than were lay landlords.

The first recorded appearance of the village names of Huntingdonshire

The dates following each village-name are of charters, unless otherwise specified.

600:   Huntingdon (650). Fletton, Orton, Alwalton (664).
700:
800:   Thurning (868).
900:   Haddon (951). Chesterton (955). Farcet, Yaxley (956). Conington, Glatton,
             Water Newton (957). Gransden (963-73). Stukeley (969). Wood Walton
             (969-83). Denton, Elton, Wansford (972-92). Hemingford, Woodstone (973).
             Brington, Bury, Bythorn, Ellington, Houghton, Old Hurst, Raveley, Ripton,
             Slepe (St Ives), Sawtry, Staughton, Upwood, Warboys, Old Weston,
             Wistow, Woodhurst, Wyton, Yelling (974). Waresley (975-84). Broughton
             (979-1016). Holywell (986). Barham, Somersham, Spaldwick (991).
1000:   Eynesbury (1000). Stanground (1000-25). Fenstanton (1012). Bluntisham
             (1042-52). Swineshead (1055).
1086:   (Domesday Book): Alconbury, Brampton, Buckden, Buckworth, Caldecote
             (south), Caldecote (north), Catworth, Colne, Coppingford, Covington, Dean,
             Diddington, Easton, Folksworth, Gidding, Godmanchester, Grafham, Hail
             Weston, Hamerton, Hargrave, Hartford, Keysoe, Keyston, Kimbolton,
             Leighton, Luddington, Molesworth, Morborne, Offord, Papworth, Paxton,
             Pertenhall, Sibson, Southoe, Stibbington, Stilton, Tilbrook, Toseland, Upton,
             Washingley, Alconbury Weston, Winwick, Woolley.
1072-93: (Inquisitio Eliensis): Stow Longa.
1100:   Abbotsley (1138). Tetworth (1150). Needingworth (1161). Holme (1167).
1200:   Earith (1219). Sapley (1232). Fenton (1236). Pidley (1260).

The chart demonstrates that many late settlements on upland forested areas were first recorded in 10th-century charters, indicating that there were no vast regions of primeval forest left anywhere in the county by the 10th century. Anglo-Saxon place-names show that several small woods did of course survive, making a heavily wooded landscape characteristic of the upland areas. Domesday Book itself refers to numerous patches of '*silva pastura*' (woodland pasture) and to '*silvae minutae*' (underwood) on manors throughout the upland regions.

Apart from place-names, little direct evidence exists indicating the nature of the Anglo-Saxon colonisation of Huntingdonshire before the Danish conquest. Almost all the land charters shown on the chart date to the period after the Danish era. Domesday Book contains many valuable clues about the pattern of early Anglo-Saxon settlements, but it can distort as much as display the truth. Nevertheless, it is clear that early Anglo-Saxon settlements were organised in a series of large estates, each estate being the size of several modern parishes. These large estates were usually fragmented into smaller units at a later date. The boundaries of the smaller units, or manors, were often used by the church to mark out the boundaries of the later ecclesiastical parishes and so have been preserved into the modern era. The fragmentation of the large estates was caused by the process of landlords rewarding followers with parcels of land, a process commemorated in the wording of some of the charters.

I *The* Bell Inn *at Stilton.*

II *Hinchingbrooke House near Huntingdon.*

III   *Kimbolton Castle.*

IV   *Almshouses and church at Ramsey.*

Evidence for the existence of some of these large estates can be found in Domesday Book. Some place-names do not appear in Domesday because these manors were then still part of large estates. This was the case, for instance, with Abbotsley, which remained part of an estate that included the parishes of Eynesbury and St Neots until the 12th century.

13 Church at Great Paxton, containing Anglo-Saxon stonework.

Several manors in Domesday Book were recorded in connection with 'berewicks' or daughter settlements that still retained some links with their parent. Domesday relates that Great Paxton, for example, had three berewicks although only one of them, Buckworth, was named. The other two were almost certainly Toseland and Little Paxton, since the churches in both settlements were rated as 'chapelries' of the 'minster' of Great Paxton.

There appears to be a strong connection between the Anglo-Saxon term 'soke' and these large estates. Domesday Book indicates that a soke could be either the rights to the profits of legal jurisdiction possessed by an individual, or a territorial concept. It records that the soke of Alconbury Weston, Thurning, Winwick, Luddington and part of Gidding lay in Alconbury, and that the soke of Keysoe, Molesworth and parts of Catworth and Swineshead lay in Kimbolton. Other documents reveal that there was also a soke of Somersham (containing Colne, Earith, Fenton, Stow Longa, Barham and part of Catworth); and a soke of Slepe or St Ives, containing Old Hurst and Woodhurst. Place-names are again significant here. Easton was given that name because of its position east of the

14 *Anglo-Saxon arches inside church at Great Paxton.*

estate centre at Spaldwick, while Old Hurst and Woodhurst are both woodland names suggesting that these parishes formed the forest pasture north of the estate centre at Slepe on the banks of the river Ouse. The sokes referred to in Domesday were probably the fragmented remains of formerly larger estates. The boundaries of the soke of Kimbolton are now very difficult to reconstruct, but the soke of Alconbury was probably once contained within the valley of the Alconbury brook. The place-name of Upton suggests that this parish was once within the soke of Alconbury, since the modern village stands on the hillside, overlooking the estate centre of Alconbury a short distance to the south—hence 'Upton'.

The two estates within Huntingdonshire that belonged to Ely Abbey (and then to the diocese of Ely after 1108) survived as sokes long after the Norman conquest. The concept of the soke of Somersham continued to exist until the 18th century, and the constituent parishes shared a large area of common grazing land. The soke of Spaldwick, described in the *Inquisitio Eliensis* as a block of land 'three leagues long and two leagues broad' survived into the 20th century. Churches within the soke of Somersham remained as chapelries of the mother church at Somersham while all the churches within the soke of Spaldwick were in the same relation to the church of Stow Longa. It is significant that the name Stow derives from an Anglo-Saxon word for 'holy place'.

Another of these large estates was once centred upon the manor at Wistow, a settlement that was known as 'Kingston' before it was granted to Ramsey

Abbey in 974. The charter recording this grant also noted that Wistow had two berewicks at Little Raveley and Bury. This royal estate was obviously granted to the abbey as a fully developed agricultural unit, not as a piece of forested land to be cleared for farming by the monks.

Danish Rule and the Anglo-Saxon Reconquest

Most historians believe that the east Midland shires, named in each case after a central county town, were either the creation of the Danes during the late ninth century, or were introduced by the kings of Wessex when they reconquered this area during the early 10th century. In the case of Huntingdonshire, the county town was certainly in existence long before the shire was created. There is a reference in the Anglo-Saxon Chronicle, dated to the year 656, recording 'Huntington town'. Huntingdon increased in importance during the Danish wars of the ninth and 10th centuries when, according to the Chronicle, it was fortified by the conquering Anglo-Saxons in 917. Huntingdon's growing importance was also recognised by the Church, and an early 'minster' was built there. This minster was probably All Saints' church near the market place, but St Mary's, near the bridge, was also recorded at an early date in a charter dated 973-5.

15 *Anglo-Saxon coin minted at Huntingdon, inscribed 'Ethelred King of the English, Osgut moneyer at Huntingdon', now in the Norris Museum at St Ives.*

However, the Danes were the first to establish the town as an important trading centre, its links with the North Sea down the Ouse leading to its inclusion within the Danish trading empire which covered most of northern Europe. The later Anglo-Saxons built upon this prosperity, establishing a mint in Huntingdon by 955. About four hundred coins survive which were minted in the town, dating from the reign of Eadwig (955-9) to that of Stephen (1135-54). The presence of three 'moneyers' was recorded in Domesday Book. About eighty Anglo-Saxon towns had been granted mints by the late 10th century, so this is not an entirely reliable indicator of the importance of Huntingdon at this time. Nevertheless, Domesday records that there were 256 burgesses living in Huntingdon in 1086, compared with only 29 at Cambridge and 16 at Colchester. Huntingdon could boast a population of between two thousand and three thousand people at this date, if one includes estimates of the families of the burgesses and of the more servile class who would have lived in the town.

Domesday Book indicates, moreover, that Huntingdon was past its peak of prosperity by 1086. Some 68 houses on the site of the Norman castle, which was constructed in 1068, were unoccupied, and there were 44 empty houses in the two quarters of the town which were not affected by the building of the castle.

The Danes conquered Huntingdon and its surrounding area at some point between the sacking of Peterborough Abbey in 870 and the establishment of the Danelaw in 886. However, very few Danish place-names survive in the county, which indicates the weakness of Danish influence here. There were probably no large areas of wasteland for Danish farmers to exploit by the ninth century. This supposition is supported by the fact that most Danish place-names in the county survive as the names of small hamlets within parishes known by Anglo-Saxon names. Upthorpe near Spaldwick, and Ellington Thorpe just south of Ellington, are examples of Danish-named hamlets. However, two of Huntingdonshire's

16 *Anglo-Saxon coin minted at Huntingdon, inscribed 'Edward the King, Godwine at Huntingdon', now in the Norris Museum at St Ives.*

17   *Abbot's Chair or the Hurstingstone Hundred stone, 12th- or 13th-century, now at the Norris Museum, St Ives.*

18   *Hundred stone at Leighton Bromswold, sited near the church.*

four hundreds (Toseland and Norman Cross) have Danish names, indicating the Danish role in the administration of the county which lasted about fifty years.

Likewise, few archaeological features remain to testify to the Danish occupation. A ditch crossing Mill Common in Huntingdon, called the 'Bardike' in a rental of 1598, was probably once part of the defences of the Danish town. A 'Viking of York' coin dating to the period 910-15 was recently found near Godmanchester.

Huntingdonshire was divided into four hundreds by the time of Domesday Book, and hundred courts met in each one to decide on matters of local dispute. The hundred of Norman Cross covered the northern part of the county, and its hundred court met at a crossroads on Ermine Street, within the parish of Yaxley. The hundred of Hurstingstone lay in the east, and its court met near the village of Old Hurst. The 'abbot's chair' now in the Norris Museum was the former judgement seat of this court. Toseland was the southernmost hundred, and a sarsen stone in Toseland churchyard is believed to have been the 'moot-stone' for the hundred court. Leightonstone in the west of the county had a court which met at Leighton Bromswold, and a square stone near the church was once its judgement seat. There was definitely a preference for holding the hundred courts in obscure and 'neutral' parts of the hundred, in remote woodland clearings like Old Hurst and Leighton Bromswold (this last name means 'the clearing in Bromswold Forest') or at isolated crossroads such as Norman Cross.

The inhabitants of the sokes, mentioned earlier in the chapter, were probably not subject to the jurisdiction of the hundred courts, since the lord of a soke had the right to virtually all the profits of justice within his soke. This again indicates the antiquity of the sokes, and shows that they pre-dated the hundred system, which was introduced during the ninth century or before. The four hundreds of Huntingdonshire were themselves probably superimposed over an earlier hundred system consisting of eight units. Each hundred amounted, in theory, to an area of 100 'hides', an Anglo-Saxon measurement of land of varying size which was used for tax purposes. Domesday Book shows that each of the four hundreds of Huntingdonshire amounted to approximately two hundred hides. A Peterborough Abbey charter dated 963-84 refers to 'the two hundreds which owe suit to Normannes cros'; and Domesday Book makes several obscure references to other Huntingdonshire hundreds besides the ones known. Several manors on the western borders of the shire were said to be part of 'Kimbolton Hundred', while one of the four manors at Gidding belonged to the 'Hundred of Cresseuuelle'. It was possibly the turmoil caused by the Danish conquest and the later Anglo-Saxon reconquest that disrupted the original hundredal system and led to the introduction of the four double-hundreds.

4

The Medieval Era in Huntingdonshire: The Years of Expansion

The medieval era in England can be divided into two periods, the first being a time of population growth, agricultural development and expanding towns. The second period was a time of economic stagnation which witnessed the scourge of the Black Death, the gradual disappearance of serfdom and the increasing ascendancy of pasture over arable farming. The first period, covering the years between 1066 and 1300, will be a subject of this chapter.

Domesday Book

Domesday Book, the unique Norman survey of feudal England undertaken in the year 1086, can be interpreted both in economic and social terms. Its value as a portrait of early feudal society is limited, however, since only the landowners were mentioned by name while the serfs were accounted for as anonymous heads of households. The section of Domesday Book covering Huntingdonshire shows that a considerable change in the ruling class had occurred during the two decades since the Norman conquest in 1066. Norman barons, numbering 20 individuals altogether, had replaced the old Anglo-Saxon aristocracy; and the church and a few 'thanes' and 'sokemen' were the only elements of the old order that remained. Domesday Book reports the fate of some of the former Anglo-Saxon landlords. Aelfric of Yelling and Hemingford, for instance, had been killed at the battle of Hastings. The few thanes and sokemen who remained were the remnants of a class of small-scale landowners, likewise under threat of eviction. The thanes were apparently of the highest social rank and the Huntingdonshire Domesday devoted a whole section to a description of their estates. Ketelbert of Washingley, for instance, had two and a half hides of taxable land, a church and a priest, woodland pasture measuring seven by 10½ furlongs and 10 villeins.

Domesday Book also refers to 52 'sokemen' who lived within the county, undoubtedly only a fraction of their former number. (This figure includes sokemen from Tilbrook, Catworth, Elton and Winwick, referred to in the Bedfordshire and Northamptonshire sections of Domesday Book.) It was once believed that sokemen were the descendants of Danish warriors, who had been given their land in the wake of the Danish conquest in the ninth century. However, it is

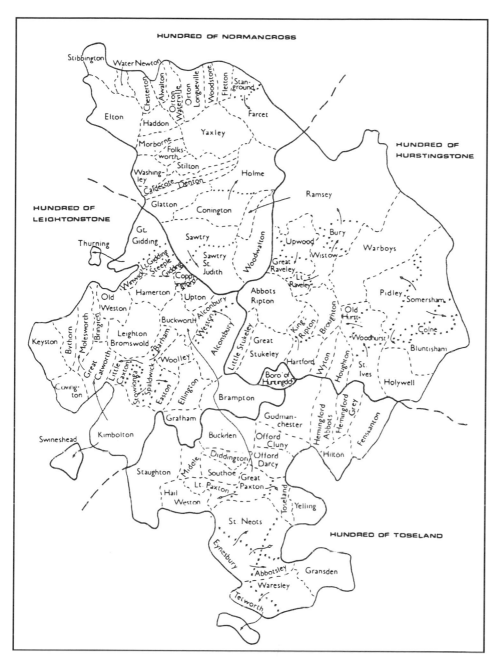

19 *Map showing Huntingdonshire in 1086.*

more likely that they were a petty landholding class once connected with the
early Anglo-Saxon estates called 'sokes'. The Domesday entry for Tilbrook
refers to the presence of 20 sokemen who had the right to 'assign and sell their
land to whom they wished and put themselves under another lord without the
leave of him whom they were'. Other sokemen were less fortunate. One of three
sokemen at Dean, just across the Bedfordshire border, 'could not assign or sell

his land without his lord's leave' while 'the other two could do this'. Everywhere the Huntingdonshire sokemen were threatened by grasping Norman barons and the even greedier Norman sheriff, Eustace. This man had apparently acquired, by dubious means, several manors within the county. One of the manors at Gidding, for instance, used to support six sokemen called 'Aluuold and his five brothers', but Eustace had ousted them from their land. Domesday Book states clearly that 'Aluuold and his brothers claim that Eustace took this land from them unjustly'.

Little is heard of the Huntingdonshire sokemen after 1086 although the term survived throughout the Middle Ages. A line of sokemen lived at Brampton between the 12th and 14th centuries, for example, possibly the descendants of a thane called Alric, mentioned in Domesday Book.

The unnamed 'villeins' and 'bordars' who feature in Domesday Book were the class of English peasantry that became the feudal serfs of the 12th and 13th centuries, bonded to their manors and performing labour services on their lord's 'demesne' (the lord's own land) in exchange for small tenancies of land. Villeins were usually seen as the more affluent type of serf. Theoretically, they held about thirty acres of land, for which they paid certain feudal dues, usually levied as farm produce. At least one member of the family had to work on the lord's demesne for two to three days a week (more often at periods such as harvest). Bordars were smallholders living off about five acres of land, for which they also paid dues and gave their labour.

However, a free or serf status must not be confused with economic success, as there were many later cases of villeins being more prosperous than neighbours who were said to be free. A villein might also hold substantially more than thirty acres of land. The bonded status of a serf, expressed in terms of being tied to his manor, could also be exaggerated. Studies of the estates of Ramsey Abbey, for instance, have discovered a high level of local mobility among early 14th-century serfs. Men from villages more than ten miles away have been found recorded on the court rolls of certain Huntingdonshire manors, such as the serfs from Chatteris who were traced on the Wistow court rolls in 1326. It was also common for women to leave their home manor to be married, and for the more affluent villeins to leave in the course of practising their trade. John Tabard, for instance, was a butcher licensed at Broughton between 1291 and 1306 and at Warboys in 1309.

Population Expansion and Agriculture

The period between 1086 and 1300 was an era of marked population expansion, as was stated earlier. John Hatcher has estimated that the population of England at the time of Domesday stood between 1.75 and 2.25 millions. It then grew to a total of between 4.5 and 6 millions by the dawn of the Black Death in 1348. Approximate figures for the population of Huntingdonshire at this time can be gained from several sources. Domesday Book states, for instance, that there were about three thousand heads of household living in the county in 1086. This would give a very rough population figure of between ten thousand and fifteen thousand people, taking into account the families of serfs and those not recorded

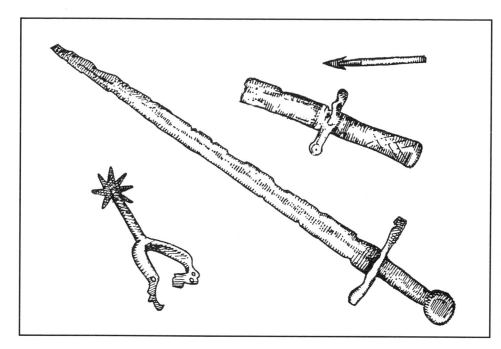

20 *Spur, sword, sword hilt and arrow-head, dated between the 13th and 15th centuries, found within Huntingdonshire, now in the Norris Museum, St Ives.*

in Domesday Book. By 1348 the population would have increased to between twenty-five thousand and thirty-five thousand.

A growing population like this had to be fed, and the period between 1086 and 1300 saw an increase in the agricultural exploitation of the available land. The Anglo-Saxon inhabitants of Huntingdonshire had established a uniform pattern of settlements all over the county (except in the fens), so during the early Middle Ages men concentrated upon developing the resources within existing settlements. Small-scale clearances of marginal land, often on the boundaries of wood and fen, was the usual rule. Assarting or the clearing of woodland became a common phenomenon in the county, sometimes recorded in documents. Sixteen acres of assarted land at Little Raveley were recorded in 1182, for instance. Peasants living on manors bordering the fens extended their holdings out into the marshes, taking advantage of localised small-scale drainage schemes. The extent of the demesne and tenanted land on Holme manor increased from 480 acres in the 12th century to 605 acres during the 13th century. Medieval technology was capable of fairly large-scale drainage schemes. The monks of Sawtry Abbey constructed a ditch between 1161 and 1179, now called the Monks Lode, that cut a course from the abbey towards Whittlesey Mere. The course of the river Nene, that used to run through Whittlesey Mere and the fens just north of Ramsey, was diverted in 1490 into a ditch called Morton's Leam that ran for 12 miles east of Stanground.

The clearing of woodland within Huntingdonshire was hindered by the forest laws of the early Norman kings. Domesday Book indicates the presence of royal forests in the county in 1086, notably at Ellington, where one hide of land was not cultivated on account of the '*silva regis*'. The entire county was placed under forest law between 1155 and 1300, although royal hunting parties only frequented small areas of woodland known as Harthay, Weybridge and Sapley. King Stephen, for instance, spent the autumn of 1136 hunting in Harthay Forest. The forest of Sapley, the name of which refers to the presence of fir trees, lay north-east of Huntingdon, and was classified as an extra-parochial area until the 19th century. Weybridge Forest was situated north-west of Huntingdon and is commemorated in the name of Weybridge Farm, near Alconbury. It survived as royal forest until the 17th century. Harthay Forest lay west of Brampton and survives in the farm-name of Harthay. Other substantial areas of woodland existed elsewhere in Huntingdonshire, notably the 'Chace of Somersham' that had been granted to the bishops of Ely in 1197. This forest or deer-park was cleared and enclosed as recently as 1762. Deer-parks within the county are shown on John Speed's map of Huntingdonshire drawn in 1610. They were located at Weybridge, Harthay, Great Staughton, Sapley, Somersham and Abbots Ripton.

The concept of forest law covered both woodland and farmland, and was maintained partly as a form of royal revenue, and partly as protection for game. These laws were resented and broken by all medieval classes from baron to peasant, and they were merely a hindrance to the process of assarting. A licence to clear woodland had to be bought, but the growing scarcity of farmland forced landowners and peasants alike to find the necessary money.

Thirteenth-century documents indicate that open-field farming had become the universal practice in Huntingdonshire by this date. The open-field system divided a manor into two or three large fields, two of which were sown with different crops, while the third was left to lie fallow as rough pasture. Each field was sub-divided into a number of furlongs or groups of individually-held strips of land, running parallel to each other. A serf would hold a few strips in different furlongs in each field, and so would have a share of good and poor quality land. It is now believed by most historians that this system does not date back to the Anglo-Saxon era, but that it emerged during or just before the 13th century as a result of land-hunger and the custom of partible inheritance (the division of one man's land amongst several heirs rather than going unbroken to a single heir). Partible inheritance would have eventually reduced the compact individual holdings farmed by Anglo-Saxon peasants to a conglomeration of small scattered strips. Growing land-hunger and the need for pasture would have then led to wholesale reorganisations of these strips in the 13th century to form two- or three-field systems. The fallow field gave each peasant a certain amount of the vital pasture he needed for draught animals and other livestock, pasture that could not be found elsewhere due to the forest laws and the disappearance of marginal land under the plough.

Early documentary evidence for the presence of open-field systems is hard to find. A two-field system was recorded at Great Gransden in 1248, while three-field systems were referred to at Coppingford and Hamerton at the same date. A large number of the open-fields of Huntingdonshire were not enclosed until the 19th century, so 17th- and 18th-century maps give detailed impressions of their later appearance.

These open-field manors were orientated towards the growing of grain crops, although Domesday Book gives one partial exception to this rule. A sheep-fold and 662 sheep were recorded on the rich manor of Eynesbury, the only such example in the county. The Fenland areas of Huntingdonshire supported a different form of agriculture during the Middle Ages. The great pastures that appeared during dry summer months were vital for the grazing of livestock and the production of hay. The marshes themselves provided birds for meat, as well as fish and eels; while reeds, rushes and sedge were gathered as building materials. Turves were cut and dried for fuel and the waterways were used for the transporting of bulk goods. The value of the Fenland marshes to Ramsey Abbey and its monastic neighbours can be seen in the prolonged legal disputes that occurred between them over fen-boundaries.

The marshes were valued as much by the local peasantry as by the monks of Ramsey. Seventeenth-century county maps show that villages situated on the edges of the fens maintained rights of pasture over the adjacent marshland, rights that had emerged at a much earlier date. The shape of some parish boundaries demonstrates the importance of maintaining access to the fens. Those of Denton and Caldecote, for instance, run in long thin ribbons from east to west. Documents dated to 1279 show that the amount of marshland held by Denton at the end of its strip amounted to an area 'one league long and 4 acres wide'. The villagers of Denton used this marsh for the provision of turves, and they deeply resented encroachment on their fens by their neighbours from Glatton and Holme.

21 *St Mary's church at Bluntisham.*

Urban Development and Trade

The period between 1086 and 1300 witnessed the emergence of several new towns in Huntingdonshire. The only real town recorded in Domesday was Huntingdon itself, but this picture had changed dramatically by 1300. Several villages were given charters for the holding of markets and fairs, which sometimes led to their expansion into small towns. Alconbury, Alwalton, Buckworth, Earith, Elton, Fenstanton, Great Gidding, Leighton Bromswold, Somersham,

Stilton, Tetworth, Thurning, Woodston and Yaxley were all given charters for markets, and sometimes a fair, in the period between 1180 and 1318. Spaldwick was given a market and two fairs in 1441, an unusually late date. A few of these village markets and fairs survived into the 19th century (Alconbury for instance), but most of them had disappeared by the early 16th century. The markets and fairs at Elton, Great Gidding and Thurning were not recorded again after the appearance of their foundation charters, although the physical location of the market place at Great Gidding can be deduced from a small cross at Chapel End, shown on a 17th-century map of the village.

A few of the villages that were granted markets and fairs during the period from the 12th to the early 14th century did expand into thriving market towns. Kimbolton grew into a bustling trading centre after the grant of a market and fair in 1200. The patronage of the Fitzpiers, who were lords of Kimbolton Castle, also encouraged this development. Burgesses were recorded in the town in 1279, and two further fairs were granted in 1441. Only one market and fair were recorded at Kimbolton in 1522, and the market had disappeared by 1890.

A small town soon appeared at the gates of Ramsey Abbey, supported

22 *Church at Steeple Gidding.*

by the pilgrim trade and the grant of a market in 1200 and of a fair in 1267. Several trades developed and the wharves of a small Fenland port were constructed on the banks of the stream that used to lie exposed down the centre of the Great Whyte. However, the town never flourished so greatly as St Ives, which was also under the patronage of Ramsey Abbey. The market place at Ramsey was built over during the 15th century.

Holme was another minor Fenland port that developed during the early Middle Ages, connected by lodes or dikes with the river Nene and the North Sea. Eight burgesses were recorded amongst its inhabitants in 1279, and by 1314 it had been granted a market and two fairs. However, the silting up of the Nene and the construction of Morton's Leam led to its decline by the 16th century. It was not able to gain separate parochial status from Glatton until 1857.

The remaining market towns of Huntingdonshire were located on the banks of the river Ouse, the river acting as an important means of transport between them and the North Sea. Huntingdon enjoyed another spell of prosperity at this time, building upon its foundations as an important Danish and Anglo-Saxon trading centre. The town received its earliest surviving charter in 1205, although it was recorded as a borough in Domesday Book. This charter stated that the burgesses had to pay an annual 'fee-farm' rent of £40 to the crown in exchange for its borough status and its freedom of control from the county sheriff. The town was ruled by two bailiffs during the course of the Middle Ages (first recorded in 1234-7), and it was not until 1630 that a mayor and aldermen were installed. The period between 1086 and 1300 was not always one of prosperity for Huntingdon. The town suffered greatly between 1135 and 1144 as a result of the anarchy of Stephen's reign, and it endured crippling competition before 1252 from the thriving fair held at St Ives. However, a charter in that year granted the town some of the tolls on goods brought into the St Ives fair in exchange, naturally, for an increase in the fee-farm rent.

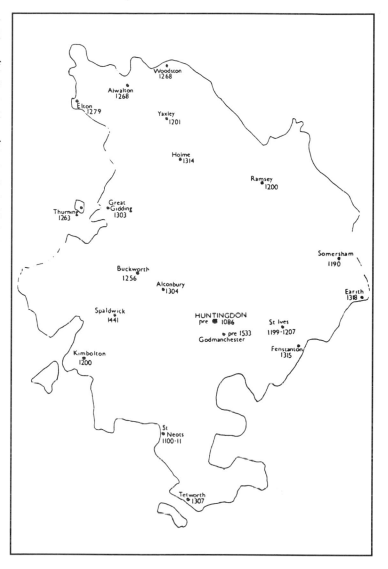

23 *Map showing medieval markets in Huntingdonshire.*

Evidence for Huntingdon's prosperity at this time can be seen in the number of churches that dominated the town's skyline. Only two churches were recorded in Domesday Book but, by 1291, 16 had appeared. Several of them had probably been there before 1086, but went unrecorded in Domesday, as did so many of the county's churches. Several religious houses had been built in or just outside Huntingdon by 1300, including Hinchingbrooke Nunnery, a priory of Austin Canons, a house of Austin Friars and three hospitals. Another mark of the town's commercial importance was the existence of a 'jewry' or area reserved for Jews, first recorded in the 12th century. The synagogue built at Huntingdon was apparently burnt down when the Jews were expelled from

24 *Church at Great Staughton.*

England in 1287. The building of a fine stone bridge (*c.*1332) to replace the former wooden structure also indicates the prosperity of the town.

Godmanchester, the former Roman town just south of Huntingdon, re-appeared as a thriving market town after the Norman conquest. It was depicted as a wealthy royal manor in Domesday Book with 80 villeins, 16 bordars, a church and priest and three mills. In 1212, however, the manor was given its first charter, making it a self governing 'liberty' directly responsible to the king. In 1279 the inhabitants styled themselves as 'free sokesmen with no bondsmen amongst them', an interesting use of the Anglo-Saxon freeman status. The town was divided into four wards in 1324, and two bailiffs were appointed to govern the inhabitants. No market-grant has survived, but a market was taking place there by at least 1533.

The town of St Neots was first recorded in 1156, and burgesses had appeared there by the 13th century. Its success was due both to the patronage of St Neot's Priory, and to its market, granted between 1100 and 1135, which was sited at a strategic point between the priory gates and the road coming over the bridge. A wooden bridge at St Neots was first recorded in 1180. Three fairs were granted during the 13th century, and the town had become a bustling river-port by the 14th century.

The greatest urban success-story in Huntingdonshire at this time was that of St Ives. This manor and priory had long been a possession of Ramsey Abbey, and it was surely a master-stroke by some financially astute abbot which led to the erection of a wooden bridge over the Ouse in 1107, and to a petition for a charter for an Easter fair which was granted in 1110. The position of St Ives, downstream from Huntingdon, gave it a natural trading advantage over the older town, while 1110 was a sufficiently early date for the fair to have become well-established before most of its potential rivals could offer serious competition. Merchants were also attracted to St Ives by the cult of St Ivo, after whom the town was named. Easter was usually the first date after winter when it was possible to travel long distances, and the fair, coming in the wake of Lent, must have been a welcome excuse for revelry.

The fair suffered badly during the anarchy of Stephen's reign, but greatly prospered from patronage by later kings, particularly John, Henry III and Edward I. Profits taken at the fair by the abbots of Ramsey during the early years of the 13th century amounted to more than a hundred pounds per annum, while Henry III spent vast sums purchasing robes and luxury goods (£1,100 in 1268 alone). St Ives became recognised as a leading cloth fair during the 13th century, but a brisk trade was also conducted in wool, hides, furs, canvas, jewels, wine, wax, crockery, spices, fish, timber and horses. English merchants travelled to the fair from Leicester, Coventry, Stamford, Lincoln, Northampton, Hereford, London and York, while foreign merchants were attracted from Flemish and German towns, and from Norway, France, Scotland, Italy and Spain. By 1220, the fair was ranked alongside those at Boston, King's Lynn, Winchester and Stow as one of the largest in England. At its peak, it lasted for three to six weeks, between Easter and Ascension. The king was probably the greatest buyer at the fair, but local nobles, monks from nearby monasteries, burgesses from Cambridge and Huntingdon, and even serfs and labourers also patronised the event. Several contemporary documents refer to labourers and villeins absenting themselves from their work to attend the fair. Local people were often able to turn an honest penny by supplying food and animal forage to the merchants and their customers.

Few buildings from this era remain in Huntingdonshire, apart from parish churches. Norman castles were built at Huntingdon, Kimbolton and Wood Walton, but they have long since gone, leaving grass-covered mounds. The only secular building to survive is the manor house at Hemingford Grey. Part of its masonry dates from the mid-12th century, making it the oldest surviving inhabited house in England.

5

Medieval Huntingdonshire:
The Years of Decline

This chapter covers the years between the early 14th century, when the age of economic growth and population expansion ended, and the 1530s, when the monasteries of Huntingdonshire were dissolved by order of Henry VIII. The coming of the Black Death in 1348 was once seen as a crucial economic turning-point. However, it is now believed that the economic decline of the later Middle Ages was the result of an over-large population, the worsening climate and soil exhaustion. The first outbreak of plague, which was followed by others during successive decades, only worsened the effects of a decline which had already begun. The records of the estates of Ramsey Abbey show that a process of contraction had begun after 1250.

Plague and Rural Society

The plague affected different classes of people and different areas of the county in varying degrees. Towns such as Huntingdon were badly hit, and parts of the rural areas were also drastically affected. Over half the tenancies on the manor of Elton had been left vacant by 1350 because of deaths amongst the villeins. In general, the population of Huntingdonshire was probably reduced by as much as a third because of outbreaks of plague during the second half of the 14th century.

This dramatic reduction in the population had a profound effect upon the relationship between lord and serf. Land-hunger during the 13th century had led to the balance being tilted in favour of landlords, who thus exacted heavier labour services from their serfs and enforced their feudal dues. The scarcity of tenants and labourers after 1348 led to landlords renting out their demesne land and reducing labour services and feudal dues in order to retain their tenants. Serfs now found it easier to persuade their lords to commute their labour services into money payments. Ramsey Abbey, like other landlords, had actively to encourage former landless men and labourers to take up vacant holdings. A new form of tenancy was introduced on the abbey manors, called the 'arentata', which commuted most feudal services into money rents. Only two virgates of land at Elton were still held by labour services alone in 1359.

The renting out of former demesne land to the more prosperous peasantry encouraged the appearance, during the later Middle Ages, of the yeoman farmer.

Demesne land was rented out in this way on the Ramsey Abbey manors of Elton, Houghton, St Ives and Holywell. The introduction of long-term leases on the estates of Ramsey Abbey during the late 15th century also encouraged this development of a yeoman class.

The Peasants' Revolt of 1381 should not, therefore, be viewed as an uprising of desperate men driven to breaking point by oppressive masters. It was a revolt by peasants who had been given a taste for a better life and who demanded yet more. Huntingdon found itself playing a central role in the revolt, being sited on Ermine Street at the crossing of the Ouse. The burgesses apparently resisted the passage of a band of peasants over the river, for which they were thanked by a grateful Richard II, as recorded in the Huntingdon charter of 1381. The king commended them for their 'good and laudable bearing ... in the late insurrection when they bravely and manfully resisted the insurgents, who fell upon them fiercely, intending to run through the midst of our kingdom'.

25 *Memorial brass to Sir William Moyne and his wife Mary, dated 1404, located in Sawtry church.*

The manors of Ramsey Abbey had concentrated until the 13th century upon the growing of grain crops. This emphasis on arable farming continued on the upland manors until the 15th century, but by the 13th century the abbey was starting to develop livestock farming on its more fertile lowland manors, bordering the fens. The summer pastures in the fens were viewed as valuable sheep grazing, which led to various small-scale drainage schemes to lessen the risk of foot-rot. This pioneering work with sheep farming continued during the 14th century, and was extended to the upland clay areas in the 15th century. By 1422, Ramsey Abbey was buying in half its corn requirements, rather than relying upon the traditional 'corn liveries' paid by its tenants.

The rising importance of pasture over arable farming led to a few early enclosures of open-field manors. Open-field farming was orientated towards the growing of grain crops, although peasant farmers did find it possible to graze small flocks of sheep on fallow fields and other areas of rough pasture. However, a few manorial lords were evicting their tenants from open-field manors during the 15th century, in order to convert the land to sheep pasture. This was not such a crucial phenomenon in Huntingdonshire as it was in the west Midland counties, but a few villages had disappeared by the late 16th century, while the populations of others had shrunk. Little Gidding is one example of a village that virtually disappeared from the landscape at this time. In 1279, 31 households were recorded there, but only six were counted in 1566. This depopulation was caused both by plague and by the conversion of the land to sheep pasture. Those tenants surviving attacks of plague during the late 14th century would have moved to vacant tenancies on other manors where the soil was more fertile than the heavy clays of Little Gidding. By 1566, the lord of the manor was grazing 600 sheep on the commonland, and the enclosure of the open-fields for permanent pasture followed only a few years later. With certain variations, this story was repeated on a few other Huntingdonshire manors, notably Washingley and Coppingford.

26 *Memorial brass to man and wife dated c.1400, located in Tilbrook church.*

Urban Society and the Development of Surnames

The general economic decline of the 14th and 15th centuries was as true of the towns of Huntingdonshire as it was of the rural areas. The decline of Huntingdon,

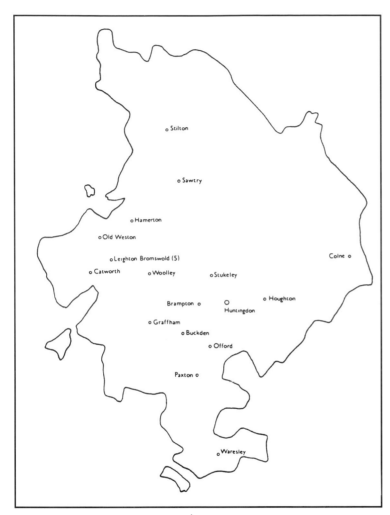

for instance, continued throughout this period until well into the 16th century. The town was badly affected by attacks of plague, and the charter of 1363 stated that 'the said town of Huntingdon is so weakened and decayed by mortal pestilence, as well as by sundry other calamities supervening, that a fourth part of it is uninhabited and the few remaining in it have scarcely the wherewithal to live'. Three of Huntingdon's churches were said to be derelict by 1364 because of the declining number of parishioners. The Ouse downstream of the town was increasingly blocked during the 14th century by mills and weirs, notably at Hartford, Houghton and Hemingford Grey. The earliest map made within Huntingdonshire (dated 1514) was drawn up to show the passage of the river between Huntingdon and St Ives, and clearly indicates the difficulties of river traffic in navigating past a succession of man-made obstacles. Huntingdon also suffered when it was besieged and then sacked by a Lancastrian army in 1461 during the Wars of the Roses. By 1535, half the houses in the town were reported to be empty and only four out of 16 medieval churches were still in use.

27 Map showing the places of origin of Huntingdon taxpayers in 1332.

St Neots was possibly an exception to the general urban decline. Market profits in this little town expanded from about £3 in 1324 to £7 a year by 1370. St Neots had, however, always been no more than a small market town. The gradual collapse of the great fair of St Ives was more in keeping with the spirit of the times. The fair suffered increasing competition from its rivals during the 13th century; Sturbridge Fair at Cambridge was able to capture its position as the leading fair of the region by the mid-14th century. By the late 16th century, Sturbridge had become the largest fair in England. Royal patronage of St Ives Fair declined considerably after the death of Edward I in 1307, while frequent confiscations of goods and prohibitions of trade made against foreign merchants after 1270 discouraged them from trading in England. The Huntingdon charter of 1363 claimed that no fairs had been held at St Ives for 20 years 'because the foreign merchants, through whose coming in to the said fairs they derived the greater part of their profits, have withdrawn themselves'.

The plague of 1348 and its successors also discouraged trade, and profits from **28** *Conington church.*
both the fair and the market had dwindled to approximately £6 a year by 1361.
However, the fairs never disappeared for any great length of time, despite the
wording of the Huntingdon charter, but they soon became trading events of
local significance only. They probably even revived a little during and after the
15th century. One indication of this was the building of the famous stone
bridge with its central chapel during the course of the 15th century. By 1534,
St Ives was compared with Ely and Sturbridge as having one of the greatest
fish fairs in England.

The decline of serfdom after 1300 was paralleled by the increasing mobility of the Huntingdonshire population. Several interesting studies of medieval
surnames have been made over recent years to illustrate this. Most people living
in eastern England had acquired surnames by the mid-13th century; these
described either the occupations or the origins of the bearers. People with place-
name surnames must have originally moved away from their home town or
village in order to be known by their new neighbours as, for instance, John de
Sawtry. Studies of local surnames have shown that several inhabitants of
Huntingdonshire's towns and villages *c*.1300 had originated from other counties
including Yorkshire, Sussex, Gloucestershire, Dorset, Somerset and Cornwall. A
man called Richard de Cornwall, for instance, was living in the village of Wood
Walton in 1327 . The Lay Subsidy of 1332 records a total of 92 taxpayers living
in Huntingdon, 33 of whom were men with place-name surnames. Most of them

29 *Holy Cross church, Bury.*

came from nearby towns such as Oundle and Cambridge and from 16 Huntingdonshire villages (see fig.26).

Surnames sometimes indicated the growing incidence of non-serf status amongst 14th-century peasants as well as their place of origin. Taxpayers calling themselves 'Freeman' appear in 15 different Huntingdonshire villages in the Lay Subsidies of 1327 and 1332. The incidence of place-name surnames was generally less amongst the inhabitants of small and remote villages. Only five out of 70 taxpayers at Elton, and three out of 45 at Hemingford Grey had recognisable place-name surnames in 1332. However, even remote villages could occasionally boast an exotic stranger. There was a Richard de London at Molesworth in 1327, a Thomas de Southwark at Denton in 1332, and a Nicholas de Sherborne at Hartford in 1332.

6

The Medieval Monasteries

Ramsey Abbey

The role of the church in the early history of Huntingdonshire should not, as was said earlier, be underestimated. The pagan Danes sacked and destroyed all the Fenland monasteries during the late ninth century, but a great monastic revival during the 10th century led to the refounding of most of the old monasteries and the introduction of several new institutions. The abbeys at Peterborough and Ely were both refounded on the Benedictine model in 963 and 970 respectively. Monks of the Benedictine order wore black robes and followed the rule of St Benedict, the father of western monasticism, who lived *c*.A.D. 480-547. Some 130 Benedictine monasteries and nunneries had been established in England by the end of the 11th century, while 374 such houses were recorded at the time

30 *Medieval bridge and chapel over the river Ouse at St Ives.*

31 *Fifteenth-century chapel on bridge over the river Ouse at St Ives.*

of the Dissolution in the 16th century. The Benedictine influence upon English medieval society was therefore considerable.

A Benedictine abbey at Ramsey was almost the first monastic institution to be founded within the borders of Huntingdonshire, in 974. The site chosen was an isolated piece of land on the edge of the Fenland marshes, now the site of modern Ramsey. This abbey was granted considerable estates within Huntingdonshire, making it the fourth wealthiest monastery in England and the greatest landowner in the county by the time of Domesday Book. The abbot was given the rights to the profits of justice in the hundred of Hurstingstone, which is why the Hurstingstone judgement seat became known as the 'abbot's chair'. The monastery was also granted a *banlieu* or liberty covering Ramsey itself, Bury, Upwood and parts of Wistow and Great Raveley. This gave the abbot almost monarchical powers over the inhabitants of the liberty. A large proportion of the abbey's estates lay within Hurstingstone, except for royal manors at Hartford and Kings Ripton, and the soke of Somersham, which was held by Ely Abbey. Rivalry between the abbeys of Ely and Ramsey might be the main reason why the concept of the soke of Somersham was to survive throughout the Middle Ages. The abbots of Ely (and later the bishops) probably felt the need to retain their rights of legal jurisdiction over the inhabitants of the soke which would otherwise have passed to the abbot of Ramsey as lord of the hundred of Hurstingstone.

The power and wealth of Ramsey Abbey increased significantly during the course of the Middle Ages, although it did suffer one reversal in its fortunes during the civil strife of Stephen's reign. Geoffrey de Mandeville, the Earl of Essex, occupied Ramsey with his soldiers in 1143, and turned it into a fortress to hold against the king. The castle at Wood Walton was apparently built by Geoffrey's followers as a forward outpost for the garrison at Ramsey. Geoffrey was killed in 1144, and his son, Ernold, eventually abandoned the abbey to the monks.

Despite this setback, the wealth of Ramsey Abbey soon became proverbial. Its revenues were estimated in 1291 at £1,310 per annum, and by 1535 at £1,715. The abbey was also noted for its great learning and magnificent library. In 1287, the monks were able to acquire a collection of Hebrew books following the destruction of the Huntingdon synagogue. One monk, called Gregory de Huntingdon, used these books to compile a Hebrew dictionary, a project which was completed by another monk, Laurence Holbeach, in the early 15th century. Unfortunately, this collection of Hebrew books was lost when the library was dispersed at the time of the Dissolution.

Approximately eighty monks were in residence at Ramsey at any one time during the 12th and 13th centuries. This figure had dropped to 44 by 1439 and to 34 in 1534. The names of the monks show that they came both from local villages and from much further afield. An abbot called Herbert de Lorraine

32 *Gatehouse at Ramsey Abbey, dated to the 15th century.*

33 *Gatehouse at Ramsey Abbey seen from the inside of the wall.*

ruled the abbey between 1087 and 1091, whilst some of his successors came from St Albans, Reading and Selby. Several later abbots, however, originated from towns and villages within the county, such as William de Godmanchester (1267-85), John de Sawtry (1285-1316) and Edmund de Ellington (1379-96).

Monastic discipline at the abbey grew lax during the late 14th century in the aftermath of the Black Death, but standards were restored during the 15th

century. The royal commissioners investigating the morals of the monks in
1535 found little cause for complaint, one of them reporting 'I pray God I may
find other houses in no worse condition'.

34 *School building on
the site of Ramsey Abbey.*

   Little now remains of the abbey buildings. Some medieval masonry can
be detected in the walls of the present Abbey School, while Ramsey Church is
believed to be the former guest-house, converted into a church for pilgrims in
the 14th century. There are also the majestic ruins of the 15th-century gatehouse, now maintained by the National Trust. Part of this gatehouse was apparently transported to Hinchingbrooke House, near Huntingdon, where it can still
be seen. The 15th-century choir-stalls inside Godmanchester Church might also
have come from Ramsey. A silver incense boat, censer and chandelier were
discovered in the bed of Whittlesey Mere when it was drained in the mid-19th
century. Experts believe that these medieval objects probably came from Ramsey
Abbey, because of the ram's head symbol on one of them. These objects are
now in the Victoria and Albert Museum.

The Other Religious Houses of Huntingdonshire

Two other monastic houses besides Ramsey were established within
Huntingdonshire before the Norman conquest. The small priory of St Ives was
founded in 1017 on the manor of Slepe, which belonged to Ramsey Abbey.
This was due to the discovery there in 1001 of the supposed bones of St Ivo,

a seventh-century Persian bishop. The site of the priory, where the bones were found, has recently been excavated, and a Roman villa was discovered underneath. The bones, therefore, were possibly Roman; whether they really belonged to St Ivo will never be known.

St Ives Priory, which gave its name to the later town, always remained a dependency of Ramsey Abbey. It later became one of the abbey's most valued possessions, because of the profits drawn from its famous fair. The priory itself always remained small, and only the prior and three monks were recorded there in 1439. Little now remains of the priory buildings on their site on the east side of St Ives.

The Benedictine priory of St Neots was another pre-conquest foundation, being established within the parish of Eynesbury around 972. It was originally subject to the abbots of Ely, but was destroyed during the later Danish wars in 1010. It was refounded shortly after the Norman conquest, and its presence is recorded in Domesday Book in 1086. The priory became subject to the abbey of Bec in France between 1081 and 1412. The later French wars led to its decline, and the buildings were reported to be in poor repair by 1439. The priory became independent of Bec in 1412 and all but two of the monks returned to France. By 1442 the numbers had risen to nine, and a prior and 11 monks were in residence by 1534. The priory was valued at £221 per annum at the end of the 13th century, and at £241 in 1535. Few remains of the buildings can be seen at St Neots, as the site was built over by a brewery. The gatehouse survived until 1814, but was then pulled down.

The religious houses in or just outside Huntingdon were poor and small by comparison with Ramsey Abbey. The Benedictine nunnery at Hinchingbrooke was traditionally founded by William the Conqueror around 1087. Only the prioress and three nuns were recorded there in 1534 and their annual revenue amounted to no more than £17. The nunnery buildings were almost entirely rebuilt as a mansion after the Dissolution, being occupied successively by the Cromwell and Montagu families.

The priory of Augustinian Canons was situated to the east of the town, and the site is now occupied by the borough cemetery. It was founded between 1086 and 1091, and is reputed to have been the earliest house established in England by this order. It later suffered badly from debt and visitations of the plague. Only 16 canons were recorded there in 1420, and 12 in 1538 when it was dissolved. Its annual revenue in 1291 amounted to £69 and to £197 in 1535. The canons were apparently living in some comfort at the latter date, being looked after by 34 servants and possessing horses and cattle valued at £58. The house of Austin Friars in Huntingdon was first recorded in 1258, but by 1538 they were described as 'very poor'. In 1336, 20 friars were in residence. The friary was situated on the site of the later Cromwell House, where Oliver Cromwell was born in 1599.

The leper hospital of St Margaret was located north of the town in an area still known as 'the Spitals'. It was founded in 1165, but had fallen into disuse by 1461. The leper hospital of St Giles was in existence by the 13th century, but was not recorded again until after the Black Death. The most famous of

35 *Bishop's Palace at Buckden.*

Huntingdon's medieval hospitals was dedicated to St John the Baptist. Part of this hospital for the poor, founded around 1160, still stands today as the building which houses the Cromwell Museum. The hospital was suppressed in 1547, but the building was saved because the town acquired it to accommodate the Huntingdon Free School. This school is marked on the first map of the town, which was made by John Speed in 1610, and it was here that Oliver Cromwell and Samuel Pepys received their elementary education.

Another small priory was established at Stonely, near Kimbolton, around 1180. This house of Austin Canons had an annual revenue of £46 in 1534. Only six canons were recorded there in 1442. At the Dissolution, the priory was reported to be 'in decay and ruin, except the church'.

The only abbey within Huntingdonshire to be established by the Cistercian order was at Sawtry Judith. This order of white-robed monks was founded in 1098, and their first house in England was founded at Waverley in Surrey in 1128. The abbey at Sawtry was founded in 1147 and the original village of Sawtry Judith was probably moved to join the present village of Sawtry because of the Cistercian rule on the need for isolation. The old parish church was still standing at the abbey gates in the 16th century. The abbey was never large or wealthy, its annual revenue being valued at less than £200. The abbey site covered 15 acres of land in 1278, including farm buildings, stables, two granges, six acres of gardens and four fishponds. The monks also excavated a lode or dike between 1161 and 1179 which flowed towards Whittlesey Mere and which was used for the transportation of building stone and other materials. They maintained rights of grazing over Woodwalton and Conington Fens, where they reared the large flocks of sheep for which the Cistercians were famous. The dissolution of Sawtry Abbey in 1536 was apparently more deplored by local people than that of its monastic neighbours. This high opinion is reflected in a local rhyme:

> Ramsey the rich of gold and of fee,
> Thorney the bane of many a fair tree,
> Crowland the courteous of their meat and their drink,
> Spalding the gluttons as all men do think,
> Peterborough the proud as all men do say,
> Sawtry by the way that poor abbaye
> Gave more alms in one day than all they.

It is still possible to visit the site and view the many ditches and depressions that were left after 19th-century road-builders had robbed the foundations for their stone.

Several monasteries outside Huntingdonshire held manors within the county, including Ely, Crowland, Thorney and Peterborough. In Domesday Book, Ely held manors within the two sokes of Somersham and Spaldwick. Crowland held land at Morborne and Thurning, while Peterborough possessed manors at Fletton, Alwalton and Orton Waterville. Thorney held more extensive estates, at Yaxley, Stanground, Haddon, Water Newton, Sibson and Stibbington. Virtually all these manors lay in the north of the county.

The abbey of Bec was not the only foreign religious house to maintain estates within Huntingdonshire. The village of Offord Cluny south of Huntingdon takes its name from Cluny Abbey in Burgundy, founded in 909, Domesday Book recorded in 1086 that 'Arnulf of Hesdin holds [land in Offord] from the King, and the monks of Cluny from him'.

Several chantries were established in Huntingdonshire during the course of the Middle Ages, so that constant prayers could be said for departed souls. These chantries were abolished with the monasteries during the early 16th century, but pensions were still being paid to five former chantry priests in 1553. These priests had previously served at Eynesbury, Fenstanton, Godmanchester, Hilton and Orton Waterville.

Other religious institutions, besides monasteries, maintained prominent houses within Huntingdonshire during the Middle Ages. The bishops of Lincoln and Ely built palaces at Buckden and Somersham. Buckden Palace was extensively used by successive bishops of Lincoln. The medieval diocese of Lincoln was the largest in England, and palaces such as Buckden facilitated the travels of the bishops round their large domains. The manor of Buckden had been held by the bishops at the time of Domesday Book, and there are records of a house and court there by the mid-12th century. The red-brick tower that still survives today was built between 1472 and 1480, and is the finest example of 15th-century brickwork in the county. The coat-of-arms of Bishop Russell (1480-94) can still be seen on the exterior. The Great Hall and parts of the other buildings were destroyed during the Commonwealth period in the 17th century, but some of the structure was restored on a smaller scale for Bishop Sanderson (1660-3), who is buried in the chancel of Buckden church. Many of the bishops in fact used Buckden as their principal residence, and a few of them, such as Bishop Williams in the 17th century, never once visited their cathedral! Bishop Kaye,

36 *Early brickwork at the Bishop's Palace, Buckden, dating to the 15th century.*

the last bishop to live at Buckden, left in 1838. The old diocese had been divided in 1831, and the palace was sold in 1870 to James Marshall. It was resold in 1957 to the Catholic church, and is now used by the order of Claretian missionaries.

The palace of the bishops of Ely at Somersham is now nothing more than a moated site within Somersham Park. The bishops acquired the soke of Somersham from Ely Abbey in 1108, and the palace was probably built soon afterwards. By 1279, the house and four acres of garden were the centre of a deer park covering 200 acres. In 1588, however, the house was reported to be in a poor state, and had been converted to a prison for Catholic recusants.

7

The Tudor Era

Changes in Landownership in the 16th Century

The Dissolution of the Monasteries during the 1530s and the subsequent sale of monastic estates by the crown led to momentous changes in the membership of the English landowning class. This theory has been questioned in its application to certain areas of England, but it still seems to hold good for Huntingdonshire, where such a large proportion of the agricultural land had been held by the medieval monasteries. The map on page 63 gives an indication of the proportion of land surrendered to the crown during the 1530s. Altogether, manors within 33 out of the county total of 106 parishes passed into the king's hands, approximately one-third of the land area of the county.

By 1600 the crown still held the manors in six of these 33 parishes (Elton, Yaxley, Stanground, Houghton, Holywell and St Neots); the remaining 27 manors had been granted or sold to different noble or gentry families, or to church bodies such as the dean and chapter of Westminster and the dean and chapter of Peterborough. A few properties were granted to speculators, who extracted all the profit they could for a few years and then resold the land. Other manors were sold to established gentry families living in other counties, while several were sold to local Huntingdonshire families, such as the Cottons of Conington.

The Cottons, who claimed to be descended from the kings of Scotland, lived at Bruce's Castle near Conington between 1460 and 1576. They purchased some of the lands of Sawtry Abbey around 1540, followed by the former Ramsey Abbey manor of Steeple Gidding by 1590. They used their new estates to exploit the mid-16th-century boom in the wool trade, and built themselves a new house at Conington. They were probably also responsible for the rebuilding of Conington Church in the mid-16th century, a magnificent building filled with Cotton monuments. The member of this family who made the greatest mark upon national history was Sir Robert Cotton, who was born in the neighbouring village of Denton in 1571. He was created a baronet in 1611 and became famous for his collection of books, manuscripts and coins. He later became identified with the Parliamentary opposition to the crown, and died in 1631 after a spell in prison. His antiquarian collection was granted to the nation in 1700 and is now in the British Museum and the British Library.

The family which reaped the greatest benefit from the sale of Huntingdonshire monastic lands was the Cromwells. The founder of the family fortunes was Thomas Cromwell, the famous minister of Henry VIII. His nephew, Richard Williams, was granted most of the estates of Ramsey and Sawtry Abbeys and of Hinchingbrooke Priory which gave him an annual income of about £2,500. It is scarcely surprising that he adopted his uncle's surname in gratitude. His good fortune ensured his position as the leading figure in the county, and by 1541 he had become sheriff both of Huntingdonshire and Cambridgeshire. His son, Sir Henry Cromwell, rebuilt Hinchingbroke as a magnificent mansion and became known as the 'Golden Knight'. His conspicuous expenditure was only outmatched by that of his son, Sir Oliver Cromwell, who was consequently obliged to sell Hinchingbrooke to the Montagu family in 1627. It was Sir Oliver's nephew who was later to become the great Parliamentary general and Lord Protector of England.

The position of the Cromwells within the county can be seen in the leading role they played at the time of the Spanish Armada in 1588. Sir Henry Cromwell of Hinchingbrooke was given the task of organising the local levies who marched to Tilbury to guard London against the threatened invasion. Almost every town and village in Huntingdonshire supplied pikemen, musketeers and 'qualivers' for this force. The two captains of the Huntingdonshire levies were Oliver Cromwell (Sir Henry's son) and George Walton of Great Staughton. The younger Cromwell led the contingent from the hundreds of Toseland and Hurstingstone, whilst Walton led those from Leightonstone and Norman Cross. The total number of men mustered in the county amounted to 914 'besides a band of 150 footmen furnished and trayned by Sir Edward Wingfield [of Kimbolton Castle] upon his own charge'. This fine display of feudal military power demonstrates that the security of the nation in the 16th century depended upon the loyalty of the nobility and gentry in the English provinces.

The fortunes of the Cromwell family, and their position of pre-eminence within Huntingdonshire, although temporary, was based upon their acquisition

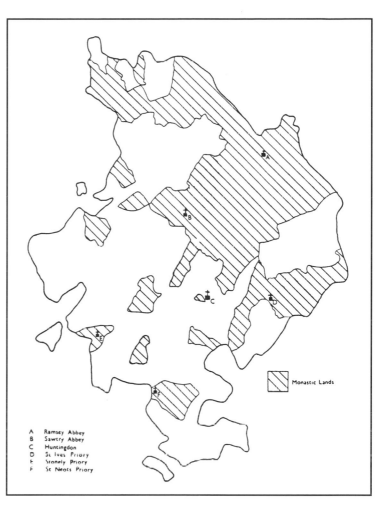

A   Ramsey Abbey
B   Sawtry Abbey
C   Huntingdon
D   St Ives Priory
E   Stonely Priory
F   St Neots Priory

Monastic Lands

37 *Map of monastic lands in Huntingdonshire in 1530.*

38 *Memorial brass to William Taylard, died 1532, located in Offord D'Arcy church.*

of several Ramsey Abbey manors such as Ramsey itself, Bury, Upwood, the Raveleys, Wistow, Warboys and Broughton. This was the original heartland of Ramsey Abbey, and it similarly became the foundation of Cromwell power within the county. It was this land which they retained after they had sold Hinchingbrooke. Their position of pre-eminence, however, was annexed by the Montagu family during the early 17th century.

The Montagus were descended from a 16th-century lawyer, and they first appeared in Huntingdonshire when they purchased Kimbolton Castle from the Wingfelds in 1615. Sir Henry Montagu, the original purchaser, became the first Earl of Manchester in 1626. His son, the second earl, became a leading Presbyterian and Parliamentary general during the Civil War. Sir Henry's brother, Sidney, settled at Hinchingbrooke in 1627, and his son Edward became the first Earl of Sandwich at the Restoration in 1660. These two Montagu families were to maintain undisputed control over the political, social and economic life of the county until well into the 19th century.

The Protestant Reformation and the Rise of Puritanism

The Protestant Reformation in England originated during the last years of Henry VIII's reign, blossomed during the brief reign of Edward VI, suffered a reversal during the reign of the Catholic Mary and was firmly consolidated during the Elizabethan era. Little resistance to Protestant innovations was recorded in Huntingdonshire. Some gentry families objected to the removal of images from the church at St Neots, but otherwise few complaints were heard. There was, on the other hand, fairly substantial opposition to the attempt to restore Catholicism during Mary's reign. Priests at Leighton Bromswold, Molesworth and Spaldwick were excommunicated for having married. Protests were voiced at Brampton, Kimbolton, and ironically, at St Neots, when images were restored to the churches in those places. Catholicism became linked in many minds with the Spanish threat during the wars with Philip II in the late 16th century, and the defeat of the Armada in 1588 was seen as a divine miracle rather than as a feat of arms performed by English ships, a view exemplified in the following entry from the Chesterton church registers, written shortly after the Armada had been defeated:

> This yeare upon ye XIX day of November it was generally appointed that there should be sermons, thanksgivinges, ringing of bells and bonefyres all to stirr up ye mynde of the people to be thankfull unto Almighty God for ye benefitt of our great deliverance from our enemyes ye Spaniards with their confederates which intended in August last to have invaded our land and to have put to sword man, woman and child, but ye Lord did deliver us out of their hands, his name be praysed, therefore both nowe and ever praysed be God who helpeth us and powreth his benefittes upon us.

Protestant beliefs had therefore become firmly established amongst all social classes by the end of the 16th century. Most of the gentry families of Huntingdonshire were leading Protestants, a stance reinforced in some cases by

V *St Ives from the by-pass.*

VI *Jubilee Clock Tower at Warboys.*

VII *Abbots Ripton church.*

fears for their monastic estates. Many of them also supported the puritans, the Protestant vanguard which had emerged during the late 16th century. The Cromwells were notable examples of puritan gentry whilst the Montagus also gave protection to local puritan preachers. The Earl of Manchester granted the Kimbolton benefice to Philip Nye, a man of such extreme puritan beliefs that even his noble patron could not shield him from exile in 1633. The local bishop also protected puritan clergy if he was sympathetic to their cause. John Williams, bishop of Lincoln between 1621 and 1642, was a firm opponent of Archbishop Laud, the greatest enemy of the puritans. The presence of Bishop Williams at Buckden Palace shielded many local men from the full wrath of Canterbury. Only two local ministers were ejected from their livings for their puritan beliefs while Williams was in power.

39 *Memorial brass to William Halles, died 1618, located in Little Stukeley church.*

Most puritans did not seriously consider forming separate churches from the Church of England until the Civil War era. One exception was Robert Browne, born in Rutland in 1550, who became master of Stamford grammar school in 1586 and rector of Achurch in Northamptonshire in 1591. His 'Brownist' ideas on self-governing congregations established him as one of the founding fathers of the Independent or Congregationalist churches. Until the 1640s, however, most Protestant Englishmen saw themselves as members of the national established church. With the new religious freedom of the war years, however, it became clear that puritans disagreed amongst themselves as to the nature of the 'true church', and separate groups organised themselves on the different lines which they felt most truly corresponded to that ideal. Many puritans were not even greatly opposed to the episcopal system until Archbishop Laud came to power.

One method used by puritans to spread their beliefs was to employ 'lecturers' in market towns, clergymen employed to preach and expound on the Word of God. There was one such lecturer based at St Ives during the 1630s, Dr. Wells, and another at Huntingdon, Dr. Thomas Beard, who was the schoolmaster at the Free School. Beard was a true puritan intellectual, and author of a well-known book called 'The Theatre of God's Judgments'. One of his pupils at the Free School was Oliver Cromwell, and the two men remained firm friends until Beard's death in 1633. Archbishop Laud crossed swords with Beard at least twice, the first time being in 1615 when Laud became archdeacon of Huntingdon. Laud tried to suppress Beard's lectureship but was defeated by the opposition of the town's bailiffs and burgesses. He tried to suppress the post again following Beard's death in 1633, but once more was unsuccessful. Beard was succeeded by John Pointer, who held the position for at least eleven years, and 'preached ther on Saturday for the benefit of the country people'. Saturday is market day in Huntingdon, so a sermon on that day was calculated to reach people drawn from a wide area around the town.

Many members of the established church were strongly opposed to puritanism. Most puritans before the Civil War era took the Calvinist line of predestination, believed in a literal interpretation of the Bible, a strict observance of the Sabbath, and the dissemination of the Word of God through preaching. They strongly opposed any church ritual which seemed to them to

40 *Interior of Leighton Bromswold church, showing the two 17th-century pulpits.*

be non-Scriptural or nothing more than superstition and magic. A contrary school of thought emerged, however, during the early 17th century, which became known as 'Laudianism' after Archbishop Laud who was its most prominent sponsor. Protected by the government of Charles I, the Laudians favoured elaborate church rituals and what they called 'the beauty of holiness', rather than placing a particular emphasis on sermons, like the puritans. George Herbert, the great 17th-century poet, elaborated the Laudian viewpoint in one of his poems:

> Doctrine and life, colours and light, in one
> When they combine and mingle bring
> A strong regard and awe; but speech alone
> Doth vanish like a flaring thing,
> And in the ear, not conscience ring.

In short, the Laudians believed that they were steering the Church of England back onto a moderate course between Catholicism and puritanism. Puritans, however, had no sympathy with this desire for compromise, and saw the Laudians as secret Papists.

There was not a great deal of support for Laudianism in Huntingdonshire, but some historians believe that the Ferrar community at Little Gidding was one expression of it. Nicholas Ferrar came from a family of London merchants that had been involved with the Virginia Company before its dissolution by the crown in 1624. He and his family left London in 1626 and moved to their newly-acquired estate at Little Gidding, where they established themselves as a family community, dedicated to a life of prayer and piety. Nicholas Ferrar had travelled all over Europe in his youth, and many shades of religious thought had contributed to his ideas. However, he and his family were soon identified with the Laudian enemy in puritan eyes. Even so, there is little evidence that local puritans actively persecuted the Ferrars. The family were to suffer from the attentions of London pamphleteers and Parliamentary soldiers during the Civil War, but some of the local gentry sent their sons to be educated at Little Gidding, whilst the poor went there for medicines and food.

The Ferrar legacy remaining in Huntingdonshire today can be seen in the churches at Little Gidding and Leighton Bromswold. George Herbert was a close friend of the Ferrars, and he accepted the prebend of Leighton Bromswold in 1626 after it had been refused by Nicholas Ferrar. This church was apparently in a very poor condition, so the Ferrars agreed to supervise its restoration during the early 1630s. A visitor to Leighton Bromswold today will notice the twin 17th-century pulpits, one for preaching and the other for prayer. This is a potent reminder of Herbert's belief that prayer and liturgy were as important as sermons in the life of the village church.

41 *Little Gidding church with Nicholas Ferrar's tomb in the foreground.*

Modern interest in the Ferrars has arisen out of the poet T.S. Eliot, the writing of a biography of Nicholas Ferrar by A.L. Maycock, and the founding of a modern community at Little Gidding on the lines of the Ferrar household. Eliot's signature, dated May 1936, in the Little Gidding visitors' book records one of his visits to the church, which resulted in his monumental poem *Little Gidding*, published in 1944. This poem appeared as one of the *Four Quartets*, and several of the lines in it are amongst the most quoted in modern literature.

Above everything, Eliot was conscious of the Christian dedication of the former Ferrar household, and he wrote about Little Gidding church:

> You are not here to verify,
> Instruct yourself, or inform curiosity
> Or carry report. You are here to kneel
> Where prayer has been valid. And prayer is more
> Than an order of words, the conscious occupation
> Of the praying mind, or the sound of the voice praying,
> And what the dead had no speech for, when living,
> They can tell you, being dead: the communication
> Of the dead is tongued with fire beyond the language of the living.

It is fitting, perhaps, that these last words should now grace the tomb of T.S. Eliot in Westminster Abbey.

Support for the old Catholic faith had not entirely disappeared in Huntingdonshire with the emergence of Protestantism. However, it had become an aristocratic religion by the late 16th century, as only nobility and gentry were relatively secure from government persecution. A few local people were detained during the Armada period in 1588 because of their Catholic loyalties. They were Robert Apreece and Ralph Haddock from Washingley; Ann Taylor from Offord; and Mrs. Mordaunt from Tetworth. The Apreeces of Washingley were the leading Catholic family in the county at this date. However, it is surprising that Robert Apreece was detained at the time of the Armada, since in 1585 he had 'readily submitted himself to her Majesty's order, and promised to furnish two light horse' for the county military muster.

A few Huntingdonshire clergymen also remained loyal to the old Catholic beliefs. In 1584 the diocese of Lincoln investigated two ministers, William Dickinson of Elton and Stephen Wakefield of Wistow, who were reported to be recusants. Only the Apreeces remained as a significant Catholic presence during the 17th century, their house becoming a shelter for Edmund Campion the Jesuit during the 16th century.

John Ferrar, writing in his biography of his brother Nicholas, recorded a local Catholic family which could only have been the Apreeces. He stated that a neighbour 'was a Roman Catholique Gentleman, yt kept a priest in his house. This gentleman and his wife came often to Gidding though Nicholas carried it so discreetly yt none

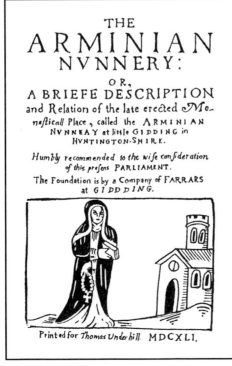

42 Cover page of Puritan pamphlet written against the Ferrars in 1641.

THE
ARMINIAN
NVNNERY:
OR,
A BRIEFE DESCRIPTION
and Relation of the late erected Mo-
nasticall Place, called the ARMINIAN
NVNNERY at little GIDDING in
HVNTINGTON-SHIRE.

Humbly recommended to the wise consideration
of this presens PARLIAMENT.

The Foundation is by a Company of FARRARS
at GIDDDING.

Printed for *Thomas Underhill* MDCXLI.

43 *Memorial brass to John Ferrar, died 1657, brother to Nicholas Ferrar, located in Little Gidding church.*

44 *(left)* Haycock Inn *at Wansford, on Great North Road.*

of hs family returned theyr visits however invited'. Even the Ferrars were little different from most Protestant Englishmen in their distrust of Catholics.

Finally, it should be noted that Huntingdonshire became the last home of one of the earliest victims of Henry VIII's break with Rome. His first queen, Katherine of Aragon, was installed at Buckden Palace during 1533 before being moved to Kimbolton Castle, where she remained for the last two years of her life. This castle forms the setting for part of Act IV of Shakespeare's *Henry VIII*. Queen Katherine died at Kimbolton in 1536, and was buried in Peterborough Cathedral.

8

Oliver Cromwell and the English Civil War

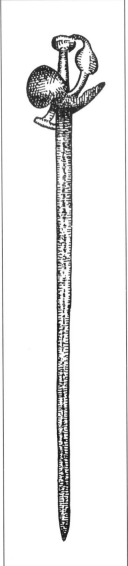

45 *Cavalry sword dating to the Civil War period, found at Great Catworth, now in the Norris Museum at St Ives.*

Cromwell and the Earl of Manchester

Oliver Cromwell must surely rank as the greatest figure that emerged from the backwoods of Huntingdonshire to alter the course of English history. He was born at Huntingdon in 1599, the son of Robert Cromwell, who was a brother of Sir Oliver Cromwell of Hinchingbrooke House. The young Oliver was brought up as a lesser member of the leading gentry family in Huntingdonshire, being educated at the Huntingdon Free School and then at Sidney Sussex College, Cambridge, before marrying a merchant's daughter from London. In 1628 he became the member of parliament for Huntingdonshire, and took his place at the forefront of county affairs. In 1629 he experienced a religious conversion that made him one of the gentry patrons of local puritans.

In 1630 he opposed the grant of a new charter of incorporation for Huntingdon. He and his friends were defeated on this issue, and Huntingdon was at last granted the right to elect a mayor and aldermen to replace the probably more democratic system of two bailiffs and a common council of 24 burgesses. It may have been this defeat which prompted Cromwell's move to St Ives in 1631. He moved again to Ely in 1636, where he inherited some property. It was at this time that he became involved in the protests being made by Fenland farmers and cottagers against the proposed drainage of the fens. His championship of a cause so dear to the hearts of many local people won him much support in his recruiting campaign in the Fenland area during the early years of the Civil War.

Cromwell was elected to the Short Parliament of early 1640 as M.P. for Cambridge, and was re-elected to the Long Parliament in the autumn. He moved back to the Huntingdon area during the summer of 1642 when hostilities between king and parliament seemed inevitable. The first trial of Cromwell's local support came in the 'Cambridge Plate' affair of the same year. Several royalist gentlemen tried to secure the silver plate from the Cambridge colleges for the king's war treasury, but Cromwell and his fellow M.P., Valentine Walton, were able to stop much of the plate from being transported northwards. Walton was a descendant of George Walton, partner with Oliver Cromwell of Hinchingbrooke in the leadership of the Huntingdonshire levies in 1588. The two families had remained closely linked by ties of friendship, and it was Sir Oliver Cromwell who erected the fine monument to George Walton still to be seen inside Great Staughton church. Valentine Walton married Margaret Cromwell, the younger Oliver's sister, and remained a firm supporter of his brother-in-law during the Civil War. He was elected M.P. for Huntingdonshire in 1640, and was appointed governor of the port of King's Lynn during the war. Walton was also one of the men who signed the death warrant of Charles I, and in consequence had to end his days in exile upon the restoration of Charles II.

Conflict broke out for control of Huntingdonshire and its neighbouring counties during late 1642 and early 1643. Phillip Stone, the county sheriff, issued the royal commission of array in Huntingdonshire, but he received little support. Parliament, on the other hand, incorporated the county within its Midlands Association in December 1642, to be transferred to the Eastern Association in May 1643. Oliver Cromwell and nine other local parliamentary gentlemen were appointed to the county committee which was to provide local government for Huntingdonshire.

Cromwell was soon recruiting a troop of cavalry at Huntingdon which was to take part in the battle of Edgehill. Returning to Huntingdonshire in early 1643, he raised a regiment of horse which was used to defend the Eastern Association from a royalist assault. By April 1644 Cromwell had raised a cavalry force of 1,400 troopers, mainly drawn from Huntingdonshire, Cambridgeshire and the fens. Cromwell's success in mustering cavalry on this scale was due not only to his local popularity, but also because the fens were used as pastureland for horses and cattle during the 17th century. Although there is little concrete evidence that skilled horsemen from the fens formed the backbone of the cavalry in the New Model Army, this would seem possible. Occasional references survive to indicate that Cromwell was recruiting local men at this time, and buying local horses. He wrote a letter from Huntingdon in September 1643, in which he referred to his 'lovely companie' who were 'honest sober christians', dependent for their wages on 'the poore sequestrations of the County of Hunts'. One of Cromwell's local recruits was possibly the owner of the Civil War cavalry sword which was discovered in the thatch of a cottage at Great Catworth, and which can now be seen in the Norris Museum in St Ives. In 1643 parliament ordered the levying of 300 horses from Cambridgeshire, Huntingdonshire and the Isle of Ely; and in 1644, Cromwell bought 49 horses at Huntingdon Fair.

Cromwell's first major appearance on the national stage occurred during 1644 and 1645, when the two crucial battles of Marston Moor and Naseby were fought and won. He moved his family from Ely to London in 1646, and thus fades from the local scene at this point.

Another great parliamentary leader also maintained a power-base within Huntingdonshire. The 2nd Earl of Manchester from Kimbolton Castle was appointed commander of the Eastern Association's military forces in 1643, and played an important part in the early battles of the Civil War. He quarrelled violently with Cromwell in 1644 since he did not share the latter's conviction that victory could only be achieved by inflicting total defeat on the royalist forces. In 1645 Manchester left the army with the introduction of the Self-Denying Ordinance, which forbade members of either house of parliament to

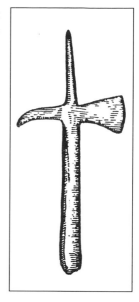

46 *Halberd found at St Ives, possibly used during the Civil War, now in the Norris Museum at St Ives.*

hold military posts. The seeds of his quarrel with Cromwell were probably deep-rooted and based on past differences over county affairs. The Cromwell and Montagu families had long feuded for pre-eminence within Huntingdonshire, and Cromwell had opposed Manchester over the drainage of the fens in 1640.

Parliamentary Rule

The period between 1643 and 1660 was a time of almost uncontested parliamentary control of Huntingdonshire. Some local people were able to take advantage of the overturn of the old order to attain their own ends. Farmers and cottagers in the fens destroyed much of the drainage work that had been undertaken during the 1630s. Local puritans were able to introduce their own ideas on church worship, and deprive some of their former ecclesiastical opponents of office. In 1644, parliament signed the Solemn League and Covenant with the Scots that led to the establishment of a moderate Presbyterian church settlement in England. Two Huntingdonshire clergy had been dispossessed of their livings at an earlier date, in 1643, these men being the vicar of St Ives, and Barnabas Oley from Great Gransden, who had played a prominent part in the Cambridge Plate affair. The new Presbyterian church government introduced an even more exacting ordinance in 1644, which evicted about twenty Huntingdonshire clergymen. The committees who supervised this work were headed by the Earl of Manchester; his Presbyterian loyalties were another point of difference between him and Oliver Cromwell, who supported the Independent or Congregationalist line.

47 *Bust of Oliver Cromwell shown on Protectoral medal dated 1653, now in Cromwell Museum at Huntingdon.*

48 *Statue of Oliver Cromwell at St Ives.*

Some of the 20 ministers were treated quite harshly, Mr. Baker of Wistow being 'imprisoned at Huntingdon jeyl where he was abused and barbarously treated'. Mikipher Alphery, the rector of Woolley, was evicted by 'a file of musketeers', who 'pulled him out of his pulpit'. Alphery was the son of a contender of the Russian throne who had been brought to England as a boy under the protection of Joseph Bedell, a merchant related to the Bedells of Hamerton. Alphery became rector of Woolley in 1619; it was a living in the gift of the Bedell family. He was evicted in 1644 and then restored in 1660. Eight of his children were baptised at Woolley between 1620 and 1636, and one of their descendants was recorded in 1764 to be the wife of a Mr. Johnson, a cutler of Huntingdon. It would perhaps make a fascinating genealogical study to trace how many modern Huntingdonshire families can claim a kinship to the Russian royal family!

The Ferrars of Little Gidding also had to endure persecution at this time. Nicholas Ferrar had died in 1637, but this semi-monastic household continued to exist until 1657. Puritan pamphleteers in London published a damaging attack on the Ferrars in 1641, and this may have inspired a troop of parliamentary soldiers to raid Little Gidding in July or August 1646. The house and church were ransacked and looted, but the family escaped unharmed. The Ferrars had only recently returned from two years in exile when the raid occurred. However, the family was known to be royalist, and they had sheltered the fugitive King Charles in May 1646. Rumours of their royalist sympathies rather than their religious leanings may been the cause of the raid.

49 *Map of Huntingdonshire in the Civil War.*

One interesting local document has survived to give detailed information on the religious struggles occurring within at least one local parish during the Civil War era. In July 1645, the parishioners of Tilbrook brought charges against their rector, Mr. Savidge, which were listed on this document. The ringleader was probably one Thomas Lancaster; his own accusations imply strong puritan leanings. He accused Mr. Savidge of many misdemeanours, including the neglect of the 'monthly fast'; that he bowed at the name of Jesus, and had erected communion rails around the altar; and that he had not shown proper enthusiasm towards the Presbyterian National Covenant. Lancaster's supporters were apparently local farmers, complaining about their tithes, and accusing Savidge of being drunk and disorderly. The rector had obviously given local puritans much trouble in the past, hauling them up before church courts and referring to them as 'the Pharisees of the times ... such of his parishioners as went to hear other men preach, and said they were like dawes [crows] that did fly from steeple to steeple'.

Huntingdonshire was strategically placed on the borders of the Eastern Association, at no great distance from the royalist stronghold at Oxford. The Parliamentarians therefore had to construct fortifications and strengthen existing defences against inroads from the royalist armies. The Earl of Manchester had established a garrison at Huntingdon by 1644, digging a ditch around the town and replacing one of the arches on the medieval bridge with a drawbridge. Similar drawbridges were constructed on the old bridges at St Ives and St Neots, while two earth-forts were thrown up to guard the roads leading out of the county across the fens. One fort can still be seen in the fields beyond Earith, enclosing an area

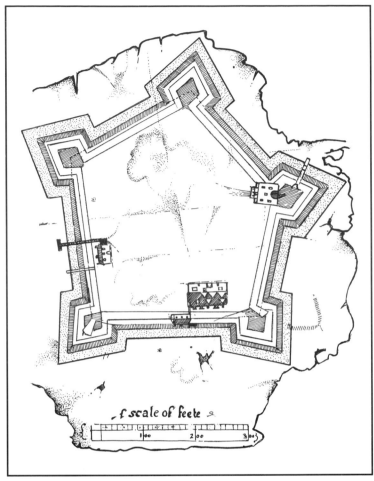

50 *Plan of the Parliamentarian fort at Horsey Hill, near Stanground.*

of four and three-quarter acres and guarding the road which led across the marshes to the Isle of Ely. The other fort was at Horsey Hill near Stanground and protected approaches to Whittlesey and King's Lynn. There is a record of parliamentary forces holding 'Hermitage Pass' near Earith in 1643, while a plan of the Horsey Hill fort still exists, showing a pentagonal construction with five spearhead projections for cannon. A gatehouse and three houses were positioned inside the earth banks, the latter presumably being barracks for the garrison.

These parliamentary defences were not sufficient to deter a royalist raid on Huntingdon in 1645. The king and a strong cavalry force attacked the town after winning a skirmish at Stilton. Huntingdon was not surrendered without a fight, and two of the town's four remaining churches were so badly damaged that one, St John the Baptist, had to be demolished, whilst only the spire of St Benet's remained standing. The king was lodged at the *George Inn* and, as reported by a parliamentary pamphlet, the town was both severely taxed and looted. The royalist force was composed of desperate men, being followed by parliamentary troops. Naseby had been fought and lost to the New Model Army only a few weeks before. The king soon left Huntingdon, closely followed by '1000 horse and dragoones from Cambridge and the Association'. Government papers dating to the Restoration period during the 1660s referred to Huntingdon as 'the poor decayed town which being on a frequented road was greatly impoverished by the insolencies of armies and free quarters during the late wars'.

The first Civil War ended in 1646 but a second conflict broke out in 1648, culminating in the battle of Preston in August of that year. Huntingdonshire witnessed a number of local skirmishes during this period. One small affray occurred near the Apreece home at Washingley Hall. The Apreece family had little incentive to keep the peace with the parliamentary party in control of their home county. Robert Apreece had become a royalist colonel during the first Civil War but had been murdered in cold blood by some parliamentary soldiers at the capture of Lincoln in 1644. This killing was apparently provoked by Apreece's Catholic beliefs, which led Pope Leo XIII in 1887 to give him the title of 'Venerable'.

Another skirmish occurred at St Neots in July 1648 and became the subject of another parliamentary pamphlet. A small royalist force in the town was surprised by the parliamentarians and put to rout after a brief engagement. The Earl of Holland, one of its leaders, was captured together with seven other officers and 100 soldiers.

9

Agriculture and the Rural Community (1540-1750)

New Agricultural Developments

The years between 1540 and 1640 are now viewed as a century of expanding population and growing prosperity, particularly for enterprising gentry families and a substantial section of the yeomanry. It is scarcely surprising that men writing during the Civil War era described these years as a 'golden age'.

The gentry and the more prosperous yeomen were the classes most interested in developing local agricultural resources in order to attain greater profits. These were the men who were enclosing manors or smaller plots of land for sheep pasture. Huntingdonshire was not greatly affected at this date by wholesale manorial enclosures, as was said earlier, but a great deal of piecemeal encroachments onto common land and remaining areas of woodland were taking place. Most of the estate maps which survive from the 17th century show landscapes of open-fields interspersed with closes or small enclosed fields of pasture. The 1648 map of Steeple Gidding is a good example of this. A large area in the centre of the manor remained as three open-fields called 'tylth-feilde, pease-stubble feilde and barley-stubble feilde', obviously referring to the fallow field and to the crops which had just been harvested when the map was drawn. Around the edges of these fields were several 'closes' called 'cow-pastures', meadows and 'walks' (for sheep). It is obvious that the Cottons, the lords of this manor since the 1590s, had been busy developing their property.

Another property development occurred on the adjacent manor of Hamerton during the same period. The open-fields here were enclosed during the 1630s after the squire, Capell Bedell, had held 'divers meetings' with his tenants. The reason given for the enclosure was that the land lay 'soe lowe and flatt that upon any continued raine the waters did ly much upon them insoemuch as thereby their sheep there going and depasturing were oftentymes rotted'.

The greatest agricultural project to be launched at this time was the wholesale drainage of the Fenland marshes. The first scheme for the complete drainage of the area east of Sawtry, to be known later as the Bedford Levels, was first initiated during the 1630s by the Earl of Bedford and 13 other 'adventurers' or 'undertakers'. Their scheme was to drain the whole area in exchange for 95,000 acres of the former marshland. This provoked a universal outcry from farmers who feared the loss of their summer pastures, and from cottagers who depended upon pasturing a few head of cattle in the marshes, or who gathered reeds, fodder and turf. There were also the fishermen and wildfowlers, and the burgesses of Cambridge and King's Lynn, who were worried about the survival of the Fenland waterways which they used for transporting heavy goods. Typical of these Fenmen was John Jackson of Ramsey, waterman, whose inventory was compiled after his death in 1685. This mentions the 5,000 'sesses [peat turf] in the Fenn ground belonging to the house he now dwells in' and the '40,000 turfes and other firing in the Fenn' which he had the right to gather. It was scarcely surprising that one local man in 1638 predicted a 'generall rebellion in all the Fen towns' in response to the drainage scheme.

The Earl of Bedford and his associates employed the great Dutch engineer, Cornelius van Vermuyden, who commenced operations in 1630. He cut a drain from Earith to Denver to straighten the course of the river Ouse, and this became known as the Old Bedford River. Bevill's Leam was also dug during 1631 to carry water eastwards out of Whittlesey Mere. The sabotage carried out on the new ditches and dikes by local people during the Civil War era delayed the drainage for several years. In 1649, however, a new scheme was advanced which had the blessing of the Commonwealth regime and which involved the use of 1,500 prisoners of war. The New Bedford River, running parallel to the Old Bedford River, was constructed at this time. The land between the two drains was to serve as 'washes', carrying excess water during times of flooding. The Forty Foot Drain was also dug in 1651, to carry water from the former course of the River Nene north of Ramsey to an outlet in the Old Bedford river.

However, this second drainage scheme was not a total success, and many problems such as shrinking peat soils and flooding were to occur in the future. There was one severe flood in 1713, while during the 20th-century floods have occurred in 1936, 1937, 1939, 1947 and 1953. The shrinking of the peat soils that resulted when the water was removed has led to the surfaces of rivers and drains now being higher than the surrounding fields. Windmills driving scoop-wheels had to be erected throughout the fens during the 18th century to carry water over the banks of the drains. Steam-engine pumps were introduced after 1820, followed by diesel engines after 1913 and then electric pumps after 1948. Flooding in the fens also had an effect upon the surrounding upland areas. Estate papers from the parish of Hamerton, dated 1756, recorded the presence of several new tenants who were 'mostly Fen men that are drowned out'.

Life in the fens continued to endow the inhabitants with an individual and separate culture from the surrounding uplands until the 20th century. The sight of herds of cattle being driven to pasture by men walking on stilts might be more rare as the marshes receded, but the Fenmen still retained the nickname 'Fen Tigers', which was apparently bestowed on them because of their strong resistance to the draining of the marshes. John Wesley, who described a journey he made across the fens in the winter of 1774, touched upon this sense of pride

51 *Fenland landscape near Wood Walton during winter.*

felt by Fenmen for their tough way of life and their bleak and lonely environment. He wrote:

> I set out between eight and nine in a one-horse chaise, the wind being high and cold enough. Much snow lay on the ground, and much fell as we crept along the fen-banks. Honest Mr. Tubbs would needs walk and lead the horse through water and mud up to his mid-leg, smiling and saying 'We fen-men do not mind a little dirt'. When we had gone about four miles, the road would not admit of a chaise. So I borrowed a horse and rode forward; but not far, for all the grounds were under water. Here, therefore, I procured a boat full twice as big as a kneading-trough. I was at one end, and a boy at the other, who paddled me safe to Earith.

The final assault on the fens did not come until the mid-19th century with the draining of Whittlesey Mere in 1853. The fens remained mainly as summer pasture until the end of the 18th century, supporting large herds of cattle and horses. Thomas Stone, writing in 1793, reported that the Huntingdonshire Fen is 'generally unproductive, being constantly either covered with water ... or very considerable parts are forfeited to the corporation of the Bedford Level, for the tax annually charged upon the land for its drainage'. George Maxwell, also writing in 1793, reported that only 8,000 to 10,000 acres out of the 44,000 that comprised the Huntingdonshire Fens were seen as productive. He argued that the poor drainage was caused by the slow passage of water down the existing rivers and drains, and that the water pumped out from the fields did not flow away at a fast enough rate. He stated that only a few acres were fit for crops. On this land the Fenland grass was 'pared and burned' in the first year, sheep were grazed on it in the second year, to be followed by crops of oats and wheat in the third year.

52 *Fenland landscape near Wood Walton during summer.*

Yeomen, Husbandmen and Graziers

English farmers during the 17th and 18th centuries were generally described as yeomen, husbandmen and graziers. Inventories—lists of property that were compiled upon the death of the property-owner—are ideal sources for studying this section of the rural community. Fifty 17th-century inventories of the goods of yeomen, husbandmen and graziers from Huntingdonshire were studied for this chapter. Yeoman farmers were generally seen as the more wealthy sector of the farming community. The 27 yeomen inventories studied show property valued at sums varying between the £560 left by William Norris of Abbots Ripton in 1626 to the £16 left by Robert Graves of Great Gransden in 1612. Altogether, these 27 yeomen left property valued at about £4,330 with an average of £160 each.

Husbandmen were generally viewed as small-scale farmers, working a few acres of land and keeping a few animals. The inventories of the 20 Huntingdonshire husbandmen studied showed property valued at sums ranging from the £418 left by William Young of Yelling to the £7 left by Richard Yewle of Somersham. The high figure of £418 was exceptional, however, and the total value of the property left by these 20 men amounted to £2,047 with an average of £102 each.

Those farmers who were known as graziers were a less common phenomenon. These were the men who fattened cattle and sheep, principally for the expanding London market. It has been estimated that by the mid-18th century 200,000 cattle a year were driven into the county along the Bullock Road, the drove road which ran parallel to the Great North Road. Daniel Defoe wrote during the 1720s of 'the drifts of cattle which come out of Lincolnshire

53 House at Wistow, dated 1662.

and the fens of the Isle of Ely [that] are so great and so constantly coming up to the London market that it is much more difficult to make the ways good'. This livestock was herded into Huntingdonshire and the neighbouring counties in the spring to be bought by local graziers, before being sold off in the autumn ready fattened for the London market. The cattle mainly originated from Scotland, Wales and the north of England. Farmers specialising as graziers became more common during the later 17th century. Three 17th-century inventories were found that listed the property left by these men: John Barriss of Woodwalton left property valued at £227 in 1678; Edward Neale of Pidley left £236 in 1684; and John Newman of Buckworth left £189 in 1694. The inventory of John Barriss recorded the presence of 15 'feeding cattle', 31 'feeding sheep' and 20 'store sheep' amongst his other livestock. These animals were probably the livestock which had just been purchased (the inventory was made in January) to be fattened for the London market.

Every inventory except one out of the 50 left by these Huntingdonshire farmers mentioned livestock in field and farmyard. This surely indicates the shift from arable to pastoral farming that had occurred in the county since the 15th century. The livestock kept by each farmer was generally very mixed. Fairly typical among the yeomen was Edward Lea of Sawtry. His inventory was dated 1624 and it mentioned his 13 steers, one cow, six bullocks, eight oxen, one bull, seven calves, seven heifers, two stocks of bees, one mare and foal, one gelding, three fillies, five colts, 270 ewes and wethers, 116 lambs, nine rams and seven pigs.

Horses were kept on 37 of these 50 farms. A few farms kept a single horse, but most of the 37 were obviously breeding from groups of mares. Generally, between five and ten horses were kept on most farms.

Oxen were still being used for draught work on a few Huntingdonshire farms during the 17th century, although most farms had turned to horse-power. Eight oxen appeared on the inventory of Edward Lea of Sawtry and six 'drawing-steers' on that of William Young of Yelling in 1628. Parkinson, writing about Huntingdonshire in 1811, stated that 'I observed but one farmer who used oxen in this county'. Almost all of the bullocks and steers recorded on 33 of these 50 farms must therefore have been kept for their meat. Beef herds were generally small, rarely more than twenty beasts belonging to one farmer.

Thirty-six of these 50 inventories recorded the presence of milk cows, and 13 of these showed no beef cattle. These latter farms were generally of a small size and were worked by husbandmen. Typical of these was Edward Kingston of Elton (1620) who had four cows and seven calves, and Thomas Bull of Earith (1665) who had 10 cows and a bull. Huntingdonshire is generally no longer a dairy county, although some herds are found on the lush 'washes' on the banks of the Ouse near Earith. Dairy cows were certainly a much more common sight in the 17th century. Samuel Pepys, during a visit to Brampton in October 1662, recorded in his diary that he went for a walk over the Portholme meadow near Huntingdon, where he saw 'the country-maids milking their Cowes there (they being there now all at grasse) and to see with what mirth they come all home together in pomp with their milk, and sometimes they have musique go before them'.

Twenty-seven of these inventories recorded the presence of pigs. Generally, a farm kept between one and five pigs but one farm kept as many as twenty-

54 *Brick and thatch at Offord Darcy.*

55 Thatched house at Wistow.

seven. This farm at Yelling was presumably breeding them for market.

Sheep were recorded on these 50 inventories in the greatest numbers, a total of 2,052 animals on 35 farms. Flocks varied considerably in size, ranging between a single ewe on some farms to flocks of several hundred on others.

Other types of livestock recorded on these inventories were poultry, and 'stocks of bees'. Parkinson recorded in 1811 that bees were kept profusely in certain parishes such as Brampton, Diddington and Easton, and a few hives could be found in most other parishes. He also wrote that poultry was generally raised for private consumption, and this agrees with the evidence of these 17th-century inventories. No rabbit warrens were recorded on any of the 50 inventories; Parkinson was himself unable to trace any warrens in the county in 1811.

Thirty inventories recorded crops still lying in the fields. The presence of these crops depended upon the time of year in which the inventory was made, of course, but the acreages mentioned were never very large. The largest amount was the 99 acres of land held by Anthony Bowland of Yaxley, yeoman, in 1671. Altogether, 18 out of the 27 yeoman inventories recorded crops in the ground with an average extent of about thirty-four acres. Twelve of the 20 husbandmen had crops in the ground, with an average extent of about seventeen acres. Wheat was the most commonly grown crop, appearing on 22 inventories. Peas and barley were also quite common, appearing on 16 and 13 inventories respectively. Oats and rye were rarer, only appearing on six and four inventories respectively.

Some of the more detailed inventories indicated the nature of husbandry practised on a particular farm. The inventory of Anthony Bowland of Yaxley, for example, demonstrated the mixed upland and fen-farming practised in this fen-edge parish. There were three steers and three heifers located 'in the fenn close' while five cows and five steers were grazing on the open fen pastures. Bowland also had 40 sheep grazing in 'ye fallow field' besides crops of wheat, barley and peas in the other open-fields in the parish known as 'the wheat feild, the graten feild and the pease feild'.

Rural Labourers

Rural labourers by the 16th century could be described as men who earned all or part of their living from wages paid by the day or week. A small-scale farmer sometimes had to supplement his income by hiring out his labour, so there was often not a great deal of difference between a husbandman and a labourer. The labouring sector of the English rural community at this date was substantial in size, forming between a third and a quarter of the population. The more affluent labouring families were able to subsidise their wages by cultivating an acre or two of land or by keeping a few head of livestock. This class of labourer was quite common in the Fenland parishes because of the proximity of common grazing land, reeds and turf that could be gathered, and fish and eels that could be caught in meres and streams.

Inventories made on the possessions of labourers were quite common in Huntingdonshire during the 17th century, and a study of 25 of them has been made for this chapter. The value of the belongings left by these 25 labourers **56** *Cottages at Easton.*

ranged between £2 13s. left by William Johnson of Offord Darcy in 1679 and the £91 left by James Elmes of Warboys in 1626. The average amounted to about twenty pounds per man. Livestock was kept by 23 of these labourers. A typical example was Nicholas Gilbert of Water Newton, who left two cows, one calf, one lamb and a pig in 1622. Only six of these inventories recorded any crops in the ground. The largest extent of crops was held by Bartholomew Squire of Ellington, who maintained one acre of wheat, two acres and three rods of peas and three half-acres of barley. All these crops were probably lying in the Ellington open-fields, as indicated by the term 'half-acres', each of which was probably a single strip or selion lying in different furlongs.

The families of Huntingdonshire labourers could also turn to by-employments. Wives and children could make an extra income by plaiting straw hats and baskets, weaving hemp, flax and wool, and making gloves and lace. The Ferrars in the early 17th century understood the need to provide employment for the local poor. In 1630 Nicholas Ferrar wrote in a letter 'we purpose to bestow £20 in flax and hemp for the setting on of work for poor folks who miserably cry out'.

George Maxwell, writing in 1793, noted that Huntingdonshire women were constantly spinning yarn. He also referred to the small lace industry around Kimbolton. Lace-making was rarely found outside the East Midlands counties and East Devon. It had first appeared in the former area in the late 16th century: pauper children at Eaton Socon just across the border in Bedfordshire were being taught how to make lace as early as 1596. Huntingdonshire was on the edge of the lace-making region, and lacemakers were generally located in the rural areas around St Neots and Kimbolton. Trade tokens were issued at St Neots during the 17th century showing women making lace. Most lacemakers worked with up to 400 'bobbins' carrying threads which were twisted around pins inserted in patterns on a 'pillow'. Lace-making suffered a decline during the 19th century, after a time of prosperity during the Napoleonic wars when little foreign lace could be imported. Lacemakers could still be found in several Huntingdonshire villages at the time of the 1851 census; there were, for instance, 26 lacemakers in Leighton Bromswold at that date.

Disease and Pauperism

All members of the rural and urban communities of Huntingdonshire were subject to outbreaks of bubonic plague during the 16th and 17th centuries, the disease which had first appeared in England in 1348. National outbreaks of this malady ceased after 1666, although later epidemics of other diseases were almost as devastating. Evidence of plague affecting Huntingdonshire can sometimes be found in church registers that were kept from 1538 onwards. The burial registers of Winwick, for instance, have an early reference to plague affecting the village in 1546. This was probably a local outbreak as no national epidemic was recorded for that year. It may even have been some other sickness that was mistaken for plague. Another local reference to plague occurs in the registers of Ramsey for 1666, where the words 'Ramsey visited with plague this year' appear. A total of 180 people were buried that year, the numbers each month rising from an average of four between January and March to 18 in April, 31 in May, 37 in June, 52 in July, 22 in August, and then back to an average of three between September and December.

Although bubonic plague virtually disappeared from England after 1666, other diseases such as typhus were still prevalent. Typhoid was found in Godmanchester as recently as the 19th century due to its low-lying position near the Ouse, giving it the reputation of being the most unhealthy town in Huntingdonshire. 'Ague', which was a malarial fever, was also common in Huntingdonshire, being a county bordering the Fenland marshes. Cox, in his *History of Huntingdonshire* (1730), referred to the county as being affected by 'noisome and unwholesome fogs and vapours' which caused sickness amongst strangers although 'the natives indeed bear them without any great visible inconvenience'. Ague gradually disappeared from the county with the improved drainage of the fens.

Rural labourers living before the 20th century had to face constant threats of bad harvests and pauperism, besides the dread of mortal sickness. A need was soon felt to provide parish relief for paupers after the abolition of the monasteries in the early 16th century, and this became enshrined in the Poor Law Act of 1598. However, the J.P.s of Huntingdonshire were dealing with the problem of poverty long before that date. In 1580 they halted the shipment of grain down the Ouse in order to feed local people. In 1586 they outlawed the practice of feeding peas to sheep so that these vegetables could be sold for human consumption at local markets. The J.P.s were primarily concerned with the maintenance of law and order, but their exertions during periods of bad harvests must have saved many local people from starvation. Bad harvests were a constant menace for the more impoverished sectors of the community at this date, occurring in at least 35 years between 1480 and 1619.

One result of the increased concern for the poor was the development of the workhouse system. Two measures were introduced during the 18th century which endeavoured to encourage the building of workhouses, while the Poor Law Reform Act of 1834 grouped parishes into 'unions', each union maintaining one workhouse. The introduction of workhouses was often delayed by many years. One only appeared at Steeple Gidding, for example, when the former Cotton manor-house was converted for the purpose in 1794.

Emigration overseas was often viewed in the past as one way to escape from poverty. Huntingdonshire was an inland county, and the proportion of its inhabitants who became colonists in America was thus smaller than that for a maritime county such as Devon. However, at least eight people from Huntingdonshire sailed to America between 1620 and 1650, when the first settlements were founded. Three of them (James Astwood of Abbotsley, Judith Parrish of Bythorn and Richard Hawkins of St Ives) settled in Boston, Massachusetts. John Astwood of Abbotsley and William Leete of Diddington moved to settlements in Connecticut called New Haven and Guildford. Nathaniel Sylvester of Brampton settled on Long Island, Thomas Philbrick of Elton went to Watertown, and Thomas Bayes of Catworth moved to Dedham, Massachusetts.

The trickle of Huntingdonshire people to America continued throughout successive centuries. Many of these people were too poor to pay for the passage, so they hired themselves out as indentured servants for several years to masters in America. Three young men from St Ives (Edward Streets, William Pegg and Mark Noble) used this method to emigrate to Maryland during 1719. Thomas Johnson from Yaxley sailed to Virginia as an indentured servant in 1721, followed by Jasper King of St Neots in 1723 who settled in Maryland. Samuel Stevenson of Huntingdon sailed to Maryland a few years later, in 1735. It is known that both Mark Noble and Samuel Stevenson were cordwainers or shoemakers, but the trades of the other four men have not been recorded.

Two local husbandmen, called James Winter and John Brown, sailed to Philadelphia and Virginia in 1774 as indentured servants. Another Huntingdonshire man called Thomas Harvey emigrated to Maryland in 1775, where he worked as an indentured servant for four years. All three men sailed to America on ships out of London, which was probably the port of departure for most emigrants from Huntingdonshire.

10

Towns and Trade

The Towns of Huntingdonshire

It took several years for Huntingdon to emerge from the stagnant and decayed state that it had reached during the early 16th century. The relative pauperisation of the town can be seen in the shifting numbers of men who applied to become freemen of the borough. Only 54 freemen were recorded in 1522 but this figure had risen to 210 by 1705. The freemen were only a section of the town's population, of course. The number of inhabitants in 1835, for instance, was about 2,200, of whom 440 were freemen.

The expansion of Huntingdon after the early 16th century was based on the development of the town as a coaching centre and as a port on the river Ouse. However, it was never able to join the ranks of the leading urban centres in England, and it never boasted a population much beyond 2,000 people until the 20th century. On the other hand, it was obviously a pleasant residential centre, favourably commented upon by travellers. Daniel Defoe visited the town during the 1720s and referred to 'Huntingdon, the county town, otherwise not considerable; it is full of very good inns ... here are the most beautiful meadows on the banks of the River Ouse, that I think are to be seen in any part of England ... this Town has nothing remarkable in it; 'tis a long continued street, pretty well built, has three parish churches, and a pretty good market place, but the bridge and causeway over the Ouse is a very great ornament to the place'. William Cobbett, writing in 1822, remarked that Huntingdon 'is one of those pretty, clean, unstenched, unconfined places that tend to lengthen life and make it happy'.

The other market towns in Huntingdonshire expanded no larger than Huntingdon after the 16th century, and remained small urban centres serving the rural community. St Neots reached a peak of prosperity in the late 17th century because of the greater volume of river traffic on the Ouse. It did not become a borough, however, and it remained under the jurisdiction of the earls of Sandwich, the lords of the manor. Leland stated in 1538 that 'the bridge at St Neotes is of tymbar', but stone arches were built during the early 17th century. Cox (1730) referred to the Thursday market and to four annual fairs. A malt mill was established in the town in 1604, while a paper mill was opened in 1804, being run by steam power after 1851. A bell foundry was established in 1735 by Joseph Eayre. This business survived until 1821. One of the most famous

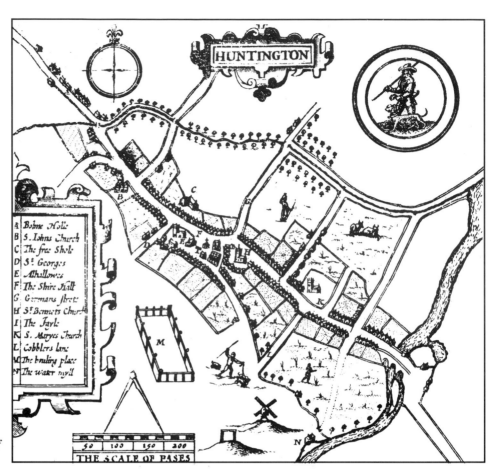

57 *John Speed's map of Huntingdon, 1610.*

businessmen who made a living at St Neots was James Paine (1789-1855). He started a milling and brewing concern in the town in 1831, besides maintaining a farm and brick-kilns at Great Paxton. The James Paine brewery is still an important industry in the town. The Vulcan Iron Works was another major concern that was established in Huntingdon during the 19th century. Its founder, George Bower, made his fortune in the new gas industry, building a gas-works at Kimbolton in 1854 and becoming involved with town-lighting projects as far afield as Australia.

St Ives also remained under the control of its lords of the manor, the dukes of Manchester. Surprisingly, this little town boasted one of the earliest provincial newspapers in England. A printing business was established there in 1716, and the *St Ives Mercury* had been launched by 1719. The *Eastern Counties Gazette* was also published in St Ives during the 19th century. The market and fairs at St Ives enjoyed a time of prosperity during the 19th century. Cox referred in 1730 to the 'very good market on Mondays for fatted cattle and provisions'. The expanding livestock trade during the 19th century led to the opening of a new market in 1886. The fairs, held at Easter and Michaelmas,

Vol. I.   N U M E. 6.

St. IVES

𝕸𝖊𝖗𝖈𝖚𝖗𝖞:

O R, T H E

Impartial Intelligencer.

B E I N G

A COLLECTION of the moſt MATERIAL
OCCURRENCES,

Foreign *and* Domeſtick.

Together with

An Account of Trade.

MONDAY, *November* 16, 1719.   [*To be continued* Weekly.]

St. IVES, *in* Huntingdonſhire :
Printed by *William Dicey*, near the Bridge, where all ſorts of Books are
Printed,   [*Price Three Half-Pence.*]

58 *Title page of the* St
Ives Mercury, *dated 1719.*

were renowned for the sale of livestock, second-hand clothes, haberdashery,
cheeses and shoes.

Cox also referred to the market at Ramsey which was prospering because
'it lies so convenient for the sale of fat and lean cattle which are much brought

thither since the draining of the Fens'. This market was also noted for the sale of waterfowl. Emanuel Bowen inscribed on his 1750 map of Huntingdonshire that 'Ramsey market is now reckoned one of the best in England for cattle and water-fowl on account of plenty and cheapness'. This situation had altered considerably by 1881 when Wise and Noble published their book on Ramsey Abbey and stated that 'St Ives has drained our market of cattle and only a few pigs are now its staple'. Ramsey Fair had also lost its prominence by the 19th century, surviving solely as a pleasure fair selling trinkets.

The Ramsey church registers indicate that some local people travelled to the market by boat. In 1632 it was recorded that four people had been buried 'who were drowned in Ramsemere as they went homeward from Ramsey market'. Death by drowning was a regular occurrence in the fens. The Ramsey registers show that in 1604 'William Goslin, a poore laborer, was drowned in Ugmear as he came out of ye turfe fen with his boate loded with turves in an extreme great wind'. In 1612 'William Feareflaxe of March, who was drowned in Ramsmeare, his boats laden with wheate, was buried in Ramseye'.

Cox's 1730 account also described Kimbolton with its Friday market and two annual fairs in July and August. This little town was always dominated by the great house of the dukes of Manchester. A map of the Lordship of Kimbolton, dated 1673, shows the castle with the little town huddled at its gates.

Only Godmanchester out of all the minor towns of Huntingdonshire was able to attain borough status during its period of greatest prosperity in the 16th and 17th centuries. It was granted its charter of incorporation in 1604, and was henceforth governed by two bailiffs and 12 'assistants'. These officials were replaced by a mayor, four aldermen and 12 councillors in 1835. The town survived as a borough until 1961, when it was amalgamated with Huntingdon.

An important cattle and horse fair developed at Godmanchester during the 17th century. Industries that appeared there during the 19th century included tanning, iron-founding and brick-making. The hosiery mill on the Godmanchester bank of the Ouse near Huntingdon Bridge was originally built as a flour mill about 1857.

Earith, with its position on the north bank of the Ouse at one end of the Old Bedford River, was able to expand as a river-port during this period. This was the first upstream landing-place for barges, and several business concerns appeared here, including one notable firm of timber merchants, founded by George Jewson in 1836. Since that date, the company has greatly expanded and has opened premises in several different parts of England. In 1921, it was the first company to sign a timber contract with the new Soviet Russian state.

The Development of Communications

The improvement of Huntingdon's economic position by the early 17th century was mainly due to the growing importance of its position on Ermine Street, the former Roman road which ran between London and York. The alternative route from London, the Great North Road (now the A1), was developed during the 17th century and converged with Ermine Street at Alconbury Hill. It is interesting to see that Speed's map of Huntingdonshire, made in 1610, does not

59 *Coaching inn at Buckden.*

mark the Great North Road south of Alconbury. A stone pillar showing the alternative routes to London (which was erected in the late 18th century) can still be seen in the central reservation of the A1.

The surfaces of both Ermine Street and the Great North Road were greatly improved when the roads were turnpiked during the 17th century. The turnpikes also induced cattle drovers, whose herds could badly damage roads, to use the Bullock Road and other droving routes to avoid paying tolls. The improved condition of Ermine Street and the Great North Road led to the development of the coaching trade and to the appearance of connected businesses, such as inns, coach-building and farriery.

The climax of the coaching era came between 1820 and 1850, just before the building of the railways. Coaches constantly passed through Huntingdon during this period, bound for London, Glasgow, Birmingham and Edinburgh, as well as eastwards to Cambridge. The names of the coaches, such as the 'Rising Sun', 'Alexander', as well as 'Blucher', 'Wellington' and the 'Royal Mail', have a fine romantic ring to them. The coaching era, however, was soon to pass, with inns being closed and coach-drivers seeking employment elsewhere, occasionally with the new railway companies. Tom Hennesay, former driver of the 'Rising Sun', was reduced to driving a horse-drawn omnibus on the Huntingdon to Cambridge railway-line during the 1860s. The *Hunts Post* recorded in May 1892 the death of J. Hampton, who had once driven the mail coach between Huntingdon and London.

Several inns were built in Huntingdon and other places to cater for the growing traffic on the roads. These inns not only provided accommodation for travellers but also offered shoeing and stabling for horses, and repairs for coaches. The courtyards of inns were occasionally used by preachers looking for a congregation, and by traders looking for customers. Famous old coaching

60 *Bridge over the river Nene at Wansford, dated 1795.*

inns at Huntingdon included the *George*, the *Falcon*, the *Crown*, the *Fountain* and the *Chequers*. Two sides of the 17th-century courtyard still exist at the *George*.

The towns and villages along the length of the Great North Road as it passed through Huntingdonshire were soon threaded with coaching inns. St Neots became a coaching town and the *New Inn* and *Cross Keys* are still to be seen in the market square. Buckden too offered hospitality to coach-passengers at the *George* and the *Lion*. The *Haycock* at Wansford still stands on the Huntingdonshire bank of the river Nene, at the foot of the old stone bridge that spans the river.

The *Bell Inn* at Stilton was first recorded in 1515, although the present building dates from 1642. This inn became the market for the famous Stilton cheese during the early 18th century. Daniel Defoe referred to this cheese during a visit to Stilton in the 1720s, when he declared that 'it is brought to table with the mites so thick that they bring a spoon with them for you to eat the mites with as you do the cheese'. The manufacture of Stilton cheese had moved to Leicestershire by 1811, but it was still sold at the inns of Stilton.

In 1646 an inventory was made of the belongings of John Braughton of Stilton, innkeeper. Little is known about him since the surviving Stilton registers do not begin until 1660, but his name with that of William Day as church-wardens is inscribed on a silver paten, made in 1630, which belongs to Stilton church. Braughton was obviously a man of consequence in the village, perhaps even the proprietor of the *Bell Inn*. The inventory records a property of 12 rooms, called the lodging chamber, gatehouse chamber, hall, great parlour, little parlour, matted chamber, hall chamber, buttery, other buttery, kitchen, kitchen chamber and one further chamber. There were 18 beds in these rooms and the linen was valued at £16 1s. 4d., a considerable sum for that date. Altogether, Braughton's possessions were valued at £230 5s. 8d. He also kept a wide variety of livestock, including three cows, two bullocks, eight pigs, three horses, 55 sheep, and poultry. He had grain in his barn valued at £33, and 10 acres of peas and fallow land in the Stilton open-fields. It is also significant that he had the right to extract 8,000 turves from the fens, vital for cooking requirements and winter fuel.

Thomas Stone, writing about Huntingdonshire in 1793, commended the parish of Stilton for running an efficient open-field system. He declared that the parish had the only four-field system in the county, which resulted in a rapid rotation of crops, because the tenants were mainly innkeepers who spread all the dung from their stables onto the fields. John Braughton, who lived about one and a half centuries before Stone's day, was obviously setting the pattern for the future by combining farming with innkeeping. The produce from his agricultural activities benefited the inn, whilst the dung from his stables increased the fertility of his land.

The shipping of heavy goods as far inland as Bedford was a major source of prosperity for the towns situated on the banks of the the river Ouse during this period. The river Nene was also navigable for barges as far inland as Northampton. The only other way, besides water, to transport heavy goods at this time was by stage-wagons, slow-moving vehicles drawn by at least four horses, while the driver walked alongside his beasts carrying a long whip. The

61 *Market-place at St Neots.*

Ouse used to be difficult for navigation upstream from St Ives, but a series of sluices built between St Ives and St Neots by Arnold Spencer during the 17th century controlled the flow of water which enabled boats to bypass the mills on the river. These improvements had made such headway by 1689 that boats were at last able to reach Bedford. No canals except the Fenland drains were ever excavated within Huntingdonshire, and so the Ouse and the Nene remained the principal means of transporting heavy goods until the coming of the railways in the mid-19th century.

New wharfs were built at St Ives during the 18th century to cater for the growing traffic on the Ouse. In 1730 Cox referred to 'coals being brought up hither [St Neots] by water', and the Ouse also carried a profusion of other goods, such as corn, lime, reeds, oil-cake, timber, iron, salt and stone. The effect of the railways upon this river traffic was not quite so dramatic as it was upon the coaching trade. Barges continued to use the river until well into the 20th century. In 1890 there were still 37 barges based at St Neots.

The Fenland waterways were also used during this period for the carriage of heavy goods. Parkinson, writing in 1811, underlined the importance of these streams and canals which served the market at Ramsey. Landing stages were maintained for this traffic at Holme, Yaxley, Great Raveley and at Ramsey itself.

62 *Barges on the river Ouse at St Ives.*

Another means of communication which developed during the 17th, 18th and 19th centuries was the country carrier. This was a system whereby an

individual from a village would drive his cart into a neighbouring town on market days, in order to shop for other villagers, or to carry some of them with him as passengers. A regular carriers' service, taking packages between London and the provinces, had emerged by the early 17th century. In the 1620s, Nicholas Ferrar referred to carriers going between London and Huntingdonshire. Nineteenth-century directories gave lists of carriers who operated on a regular basis out of almost every village in Huntingdonshire, travelling to local towns such as Huntingdon and Peterborough. John Savage of Glatton, for instance, was recorded in a directory of 1890 as a carrier who visited Peterborough on Wednesdays and Saturdays. A carrier usually maintained other sources of income besides his occasional expeditions to local towns. John Parnell of Winwick travelled regularly to Huntingdon as a carrier, but in 1837 he also kept 26 sheep on land at Brington. Carriers remained an important part of rural life until well into the 20th century when they were gradually replaced by motor buses. The first motor bus in Huntingdonshire was apparently that operating between Huntingdon and St Neots in 1913.

Local Industries and Trades

Huntingdonshire was never an important cloth-producing area in comparison with some other parts of East Anglia. Peterborough and Stamford were both important cloth towns until the late 18th century but the towns of Huntingdonshire were never renowned for their role in this great industry. Many rural families in the county supplemented their incomes by spinning and preparing wool for cloth merchants, but Huntingdonshire was more important as a source of raw wool for cloth towns elsewhere. For this reason, towns such as Huntingdon sold wool at their fairs and markets to cloth merchants from neighbouring counties.

One local trade which has not received much attention was the sale of fish caught in the rivers and meres of the fens. In 1730 Cox mentioned this source of food which 'maintain many families in getting them, and carrying them to the Gentry and Markets in this county and Cambridge'. Daniel Defoe referred in the 1720s to the fish trade practised between the fens and the London markets, particularly 'a trade ... for carrying fish alive by land carriage; this they do by carrying great butts filled with water in waggons, as the carriers draw other goods ... in these carriages they chiefly carry especially tench and pike, of which here are some of the largest in England'. Inventories can sometimes be found which record the belongings of fishermen living in the fens. William Barton of Holme, fisherman, left an inventory in 1647 that refers to his fishing nets, besides the cow and calf that he grazed on the Fenland pastures.

One sign of the growing prosperity of Huntingdon during the 18th century was the development of a banking system within the town. John Pasheller founded the first bank in 1727, but it was eventually bought by the firm of Rust and Veasey, established in 1793. Another early bank was that founded by John Perkins, but this went bankrupt in 1805.

Finally, the close links between craftsmen and the agricultural world at this date should be emphasised. Few town craftsmen were so preoccupied with

63 *St Mary's church at St Neots.*

their trades that they neglected to keep a few head of livestock or maintain a small acreage of crops. A study of some twenty 17th-century inventories left by Huntingdonshire craftsmen has shown that only one of them did not keep any livestock at all, whilst eight of them grew a few acres of crops. Edward Key of Godmanchester, glover, was typical. His inventory of 1684 recorded three cows, two pigs and four acres of wheat, rye, and barley.

VIII *Clock tower at Fenstanton.*

IX *Chinese bridge at Godmanchester.*

X *River Ouse at Hemingford Grey.*

11

The County Community of Gentry

The Nobility and Gentry

The political, economic and social life of the county of Huntingdonshire was dominated by aristocratic and gentry families until the late 19th century. Many English counties supported one or two hundred different gentry families, a great 'cousinage' which inter-married amongst itself, supplied virtually all the candidates for the post of justice of the peace, and upon whose loyalty depended the survival of the government in London. Some historians have argued, for instance, that the shifting allegiances of the county gentry controlled the rise and fall of the parliamentary side during the Civil War. The gentry also virtually monopolised advanced education at the universities and Inns of Court, and they owned most of the estates in each county, besides maintaining interests in local trades and industries. Their power over their social inferiors was exercised only on rare occasions. Generally, it rested upon the traditional respect felt by farmers and labourers towards them. Samuel Pepys recorded a fine example of this traditional respect when he attended a Cambridgeshire church with his country cousins in August 1661: 'To church, and had a good plain sermon. At our

64 *Kimbolton Castle c.1933-34.*

65 *Hinchingbrooke House near Huntingdon.*

coming-in, the country-people all rose with so much reverence; and when the parson begins, he begins "Right worshipfull and dearly beloved" to us'.

The concept of a county community of gentry is particularly valid for the larger counties which contained few great aristocratic families. The gentry in Kent and Cornwall, for instance, maintained an almost undisputed control over local affairs. This was not the case with Huntingdonshire, where a resident aristocratic family controlled the destinies of a geographically small county. The Montagus of Hinchingbrooke and Kimbolton Castle could manipulate the ambitions of many local gentry families. The latter were either occupied with their own estates, or paid court to the Montagus in the hope of attaining local office.

The two branches of the Montagu family had emerged with their fortunes largely intact upon the restoration of Charles II in 1660. The 2nd Earl of Manchester, who had fought for parliament during the Civil War, had become an opponent of the Cromwellian regime by the late 1640s. He was made Lord Chamberlain at the Restoration and died in 1671. Charles, the 4th Earl of Manchester, was created Duke of Manchester in 1719. His successors lived at Kimbolton Castle until 1950.

The branch of the Montagus living at Hinchingbrooke House became even more influential after the Restoration. Sir Sidney Montagu, the original purchaser of Hinchingbrooke, became a royalist during the war but died in 1644. His son, Edward, was a parliamentarian and a colonel in the New Model Army. He was an admirer of Cromwell, even to the extent of supporting him in his quarrel with the Earl of Manchester. Edward Montagu fought at Marston Moor and Naseby, and served as a member of the Long and Protectorate parliaments. He was appointed Commander of the Baltic Fleet, but turned to the royalist cause upon Cromwell's death in 1658, and was instrumental in the Restoration of Charles II. He was created Earl of Sandwich for this service, and became an admiral in the navy, eventually being killed in 1672 whilst fighting the Dutch.

Sandwich is now mainly remembered as the patron of Samuel Pepys, the great diarist. The Pepys family originated from Cottenham in the Cambridgeshire fens, but Samuel was born in London, the son of a tailor. One of his relations, Paulina Pepys, was married to Sir Sidney Montagu, which explains the connection between Samuel and Sir Sidney's son. Pepys lived at Brampton for part of his boyhood, and attended the Huntingdon Free School. He became Montagu's secretary in 1660, after serving him in more minor capacities. Pepys

66 Aerial view of Hinchingbrooke House.

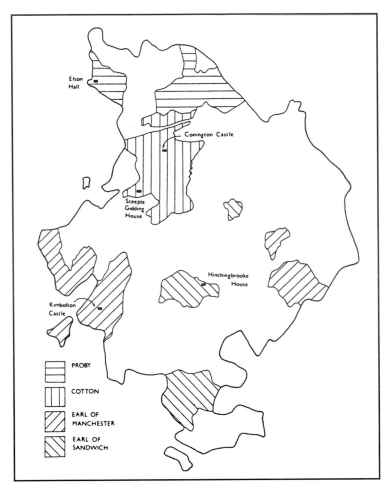

67 *Map showing major estates in Huntingdonshire in 1750.*

often visited Hinchingbrooke in later life, and maintained many links with Huntingdonshire families. His parents were buried at Brampton, and his sister Pall was married in 1668 to John Jackson, a grazier from Ellington. Pepys mentioned his sister in his diary in May 1668 whilst he was in Brampton: 'I saw my brother and sister Jackson ... they are going shortly to live at Ellington of themselfs, and will keep malting and grazing of cattle'.

The family of the earls of Sandwich continued to live at Hinchingbrooke until 1964, when the successor to the ninth earl relinquished the title and sold the house. Edward Montagu's most famous successor was the fourth earl, who became First Lord of the Admiralty and after whom the Sandwich Islands were named. He was also a notorious gambler and is reputed to have invented the 'sandwich' as a means of eating meals without leaving the gaming tables.

The number of gentry families living in Huntingdonshire was a great deal smaller than that in some other counties. A Herald's Visitation made to the county in 1613 to check the claims of local families to bear arms recorded the presence of 60 families that boasted this right. A map of Huntingdonshire drawn up in 1750 by Emanuel Bowen named 35 families that owned mansion houses within the county. Parkinson, writing in 1811, referred to 36 'principal' houses in the county owned by nobility and gentry.

Some of the 60 armigerous families recorded in 1613 were wealthy and famous, including the St Johns of Kings Ripton, the Cliftons of Leighton Bromswold, the Cottons of Conington, the Cromwells of Hinchingbrooke and Upwood, and the Wingfields of Kimbolton Castle. Another great gentry family was that of the Dyers of Great Staughton, whose magnificent monuments can still be seen in the parish church. The earliest one is to Sir James Dyer, who became Speaker of the House of Commons in 1558, and Lord Chief Justice of the Common Pleas. The adjacent monument is to his great-nephew, Sir Richard Dyer, who became a Gentleman of the Privy Chamber to James I. Another notable gentry family living in Huntingdonshire at this date was that of the Drydens of Chesterton House. They were related to John Dryden

(1631-1700), the great Restoration poet, who was born at Aldwinkle in Northamptonshire.

The arrival of the Montagus at Kimbolton Castle by 1615 and at Hinchingbrooke by 1627 considerably altered the nature of the county community of gentry. The 1750 map made by Emanuel Bowen indicates this, showing the earls of Manchester as lords of the manors of Great Catworth, Covington, Keyston, Kimbolton, Spaldwick, Stow Longa, Swineshead, Holywell, Old Hurst and St Ives. The earls of Sandwich possessed only four Huntingdonshire manors, although three of these were the wealthy ones of St Neots, Eynesbury and Brampton. Their fourth manor was at Little Raveley. Both branches of the Montagus also possessed land in other counties.

The 1750 map shows that the Cromwell family had disappeared from the county by this date, although some Cromwells continued to live in the Ramsey area until the late 17th century. Some of them reverted to their original surname of Williams in order to conceal their links with their great ancestor. Samuel Pepys records meeting a Colonel Williams at Hinchingbrooke House in September 1663, one of Cromwell's cousins who had changed his name at the Restoration.

Several other pre-Civil War families were still resident in the county in 1750. The Ferrars were still at Little Gidding, and the Apreeces at Washingley. The Cottons were also still recorded, one branch at Conington and another at Steeple Gidding. These two families were the greatest county landowners after the Montagus, holding the manors of Conington, Denton, Steeple Gidding, Glatton, Sawtry St Andrew, Sawtry Judith, Stilton and Upton. Another major gentry family was that of the Probys of Elton Hall, who held the manors of Elton, Farcet, Fletton and Yaxley. They had bought their home estate of Elton, the former Ramsey Abbey manor, direct from the crown in 1624. Elton Hall, originally the home of the Sapcotes, was rebuilt by the Probys during the 1660s. John Proby, M.P. for Huntingdonshire between 1754 and 1768, was created Baron Carysfort in 1752, and his son John became the first earl of Carysfort in 1789. These were originally Irish titles, thus allowing the first John to hold his seat in the House of Commons, but the second John entered the English peerage in 1801 when he was created Baron Carysfort of Norman Cross. This last Proby gave important support to William Wilberforce's campaign for the abolition of slavery.

The other resident gentry families of Huntingdonshire held only one or two manors each, or none at all. The greater of these were the Hammonds of Somersham, the Dunscombes of Buckworth, the Handasys of Gains Hall, the Biggs of Grafham, the Mitchells of Hemingford Grey and the Pigots of Chesterton.

Parkinson's list of Huntingdonshire mansions drawn up in 1811 again shows considerable changes amongst the county gentry. The Montagus were still at Kimbolton and Hinchingbrooke, but most of the great names of the past had disappeared. There were no Cottons at Conington and Steeple Gidding, no Ferrars at Little Gidding, and no Apreeces at Washingley. Another aristocratic family had appeared—the earls of Aboyne, who had two mansion houses at Chesterton and at Orton Longueville.

68 *Church at Little Gidding.*

By 1873, the supremacy of the Montagus was apparently being contested by a successor of the Cromwells of Ramsey. The *Return of Owners of Land* made in that year shows that some 16 landowners living in Huntingdonshire owned more than 1,000 acres of land. Another 20 landowners (who included the railway companies, the crown, the Cambridge colleges and the Ecclesiastical Commissioners) owned over 1,000 acres but lived outside the borders of Huntingdonshire. Among the 16 resident landowners were three aristocrats: the Duke of Manchester who owned 13,835 acres in the county; the Earl of Sandwich with 3,219 acres; and the Earl of Carysfort who owned 3,654 acres. However, the greatest owner of land resident in Huntingdonshire was now Edward Fellowes of Ramsey Abbey, who owned a total of 15,629 acres. The last male member of the Cromwell family who held property in the Ramsey area was Henry Cromwell, who died in 1673. His estates were purchased by a Colonel Titus around 1674, and Coulson Fellowes bought the manor of Ramsey *c.*1736. Edward Fellowes was the great-grandson of Coulson, and was later created first Baron de Ramsey. The clock in the centre of the Great Whyte at Ramsey was erected in 1888 as a memorial to him.

Lady Olivia Bernard Sparrow was another member of the Huntingdonshire gentry to make her mark during the course of the 19th century. She was widowed in 1805 and inherited the estates of the Bernard family of Brampton Hall. She became a great benefactress in the Huntingdon area, and estate cottages bearing the initials 'O.B.S.' can still be seen in Brampton and elsewhere. She died in 1863 and was buried in Brampton church.

Some local gentry families acquired reputations that extended far beyond the borders of Huntingdonshire. The activities of the Gunnings of Hemingford Grey, for instance, led to the introduction of Lord Hardwicke's Marriage Act in 1754. Mary and Elizabeth, the daughters of John Gunning, were baptised at Hemingford Grey in 1732 and 1733 respectively, Their father had originated from Ireland but was related to the Mitchells of Hemingford Grey. He rented the manor house from William Mitchell between 1731 and 1741. The two girls became notorious beauties and were clandestinely married in 1752 to the earl of Coventry and the duke of Hamilton. The Hemingford church registers record

69 *Manor house at Hilton.*

these marriages underneath the girls' baptism entries. The marriage of Elizabeth to the duke of Hamilton took place without banns, licence or ring, and the ensuing scandal induced Lord Hardwicke to introduce his bill as an attempt to prevent such clandestine marriages. The new church marriage registers of 1754 were the most important result of this act, and the additional information on marriages thus provided has benefited many later generations of historians and genealogists.

Another family which joined the ranks of the Huntingdonshire gentry has left its mark as much on the English landscape as in English history. Lancelot 'Capability' Brown, the famous landscape gardener, was never given any major commissions within Huntingdonshire, but in 1768 he was granted the manor of Fenstanton with Hilton by the earl of Northampton to settle an old debt. He was soon accepted within the county community of gentry, despite his humble origins. He was appointed High Sheriff of the County in 1770, while his son (another Lancelot) became M.P. for Huntingdon. Lancelot senior died at Fenstanton in 1783 and his memorial can be seen in the village church. His son continued to live at Fenstanton as lord of the manor after his father's death.

J.P.s and Quarter Sessions

The position of the gentry as the ruling group in the county under the Montagus was supported by their monopoly of local government positions. The office of justice of the peace had emerged during the later Middle Ages, and had been extended during the 16th century to cover a wide range of duties, many of which had previously been undertaken by the county sheriff. There were 37 J.P.s recorded for Huntingdonshire in 1659, and there was keen competition among the local gentry to attain this office. Their duties included the maintenance of law and order; the control of labourers and the local poor; the regulation of prices and wages; the maintenance of bridges and roads; the licensing of ale-

70 *Unusual wooden tower on church at Hail Weston.*

houses; and the administration of the anti-Catholic recusancy laws. In short, the county's J.P.s supervised almost all aspects of local government, under the very loose controls exercised by the central government.

The Huntingdonshire J.P.s met together four times a year at the quarter sessions, usually held in the Court House at Huntingdon. A great deal of work was otherwise carried out by most J.P.s in their private homes, and they themselves relied upon a network of parish officials, usually drawn from the yeoman class, in such offices as constables, overseers of the poor, churchwardens and surveyors of the highways. These were the men who extended the work of the J.P.s down to the parish level.

The earliest quarter sessions minute books to survive for Huntingdonshire commence in 1782. The names of the J.P.s attending each sessions were given, and a study of these names at the 16 sessions held between January 1782 and October 1785 shows that varying numbers of them attended each sessions. There were 15 J.P.s at the sessions in October 1785, while only three attended that in April 1783. The office of J.P. may have seemed an empty honour to a certain section of local gentry, who were content to leave most of the work to a dedicated few. The most industrious J.P.s during the period examined were the Reverend Matthew Maddock, Eustace Kentish and John Jackson, who each attended nine out of 16 sessions. It is interesting to see that there were as many as six Anglican ministers among the 21 J.P.s who attended at least one of the sessions between 1782 and 1785. The county's ruling family was also well represented by the Earl of Sandwich (who attended seven sessions), Viscount Hinchingbrooke (four sessions) and the Earl of Manchester (two sessions). Another famous name amongst these 21 J.P.s was that of Lancelot, the son of 'Capability' Brown, who attended six sessions.

Local magnates, such as the Montagus, were able to maintain their influence over the local gentry by sponsoring the latter's applications for local official positions. J.P.s were theoretically appointed by the central government, but a great deal of pressure could be exerted by a nobleman to secure the appointment of his own candidates. The Montagus could also exert power through their seats in the House of Lords, and by influencing the elections of local members of parliament. The death of Henry Cromwell in 1673 was apparently caused by his fury over the failure of his own candidate to defeat the man sponsored by the Earl of Manchester in the general election of that year.

The first record of M.P.s being sent to parliament from Huntingdonshire occurs in 1290. Two were sent by the county itself and two by the borough of Huntingdon. The number of electors in the county at any one time was relatively small (494 men in 1490, for instance), and the situation did not improve a great deal before the parliamentary reforms of the 19th century. The borough of Huntingdon maintained its right to two M.P.s until 1867, when it lost one of them. In 1887 this borough constituency was amalgamated with the county, and henceforth there was only one M.P. for Huntingdonshire.

The Huntingdonshire constituency has been served by two distinguished Conservative M.P.s during recent years. David Renton was elected to the seat in the 1945 general election. He served in the government at the Ministry of Power and in the Home Office between 1955 and 1962. He was knighted in 1964 and made a life peer on his retirement from the Commons in 1979.

John Major succeeded him as M.P. for Huntingdonshire in 1979 and, following boundary changes in 1983, for the Huntingdon constituency. Mr. Major became Parliamentary Under Secretary of State at the Department of Health and Social Security in 1985, Minister of State in 1986, Chief Secretary to the Treasury in 1987 and Foreign Secretary in July 1989. He only served in the Foreign and Commonwealth Office for a few months, however, before being appointed Chancellor of the Exchequer in October 1989. He became Prime Minister in November 1990.

Social Activities of the Gentry

One centre of political and social life for the Huntingdonshire gentry was the Court House at Huntingdon. The present hall was built in 1744 to replace the building which is shown on John Speed's map of the town in 1610. The Assembly Room on the second floor was in constant demand for social functions, including playing cards and drinking tea. The local gentry also met for outdoor activities, such as fox-hunting and horse-racing. The racecourse on the Port Holme meadow just outside Huntingdon was established during the 18th century, and was referred to by William Cobbett in 1822. Cobbett also mentioned the bowling-green at Huntingdon, possibly the same as that shown on Speed's map. The poet William Cowper, who came to live in Huntingdon in 1765, referred in a letter to pastimes in the town, such as 'a card-assembly, and a dancing-assembly, and a horse race, and a club, and a bowling-green'.

William Hopkinson (1755-1821) was a fine example of a late 18th-century fox-hunting squire. He came from Sutton Grange near Wansford and was a member of the Fitzwilliam Hunt. He wrote a hunting diary between 1787 and 1804, and recorded one hunt in December 1787, which commenced at

71 Village green and earth maze at Hilton.

Coppingford, went through Upton and Monk's Wood and ended at Stukeley. The Fitzwilliam Hunt apparently ranged over a large area of Huntingdonshire. The *Hunts Post* in February 1908 recorded one hunt where the unfortunate fox was actually chased through the streets of Huntingdon!

Another sport followed by the gentry during the 19th century was that of boating on Whittlesey Mere, the Fenland lake, which was not drained until 1853. The mere was over two miles across and covered some 1,500 acres. Boat-houses, a bandstand and refreshment booths were built on its shores, while yacht races and regattas were held on the water. The mere was also frequented by ice-skaters in winter. Skating was a sport widely practised in the fens by all classes, since it was a practical way of travelling across the marshes in the depths of winter. The original skates were made from the leg bones of sheep, and metal runners were only introduced later. Fine examples of Fenland skates can be seen in the Norris Museum at St Ives. The first recorded skating matches held in the fens were in 1820, usually in the form of two-mile races up and down the long Fenland dikes. Fenmen remained as English skating champions until as recently as 1930.

12

Religious Dissent

Dissent 1660-1750

England experienced a religious revolution during the period between 1640 and 1660. The established church lost its supreme position and a variety of churches and sects strove for dominance. A Presbyterian church system was adopted by parliament in 1644, but it never really took root. The royalists allied themselves with noted Presbyterians such as the Earl of Manchester during the Commonwealth era, but it was Anglicanism and not Presbyterianism that was restored in 1660, shorn only of the more repressive institutions of Laudianism. This led to the ejection of at least eleven ministers of sectarian inclination from Huntingdonshire parishes.

In contrast, ejected Anglican ministers were reinstated. In Huntingdonshire, the clerics so restored included Mikepher Alphery of Woolley and Barnabas Oley of Great Gransden. Oley continued to live at Great Gransden until his death in 1685, and founded a school there about 1670. There is still a plaque in the parish church to his memory.

The years between the Act of Uniformity in 1662 and the Declaration of Indulgence in 1672 were years of persecution for those Protestant dissenters who could not accept the restored Anglican church. One example was John Bunyan, the great nonconformist writer, who was imprisoned at Bedford between 1660 and 1672. Despite this persecution, however, dissenters remained in considerable numbers in parts of Huntingdonshire during this period, one observer reporting in 1664 that only 20 out of the 400 families living in Huntingdon were Anglican communicants.

Several of the puritan ministers ejected in 1662 founded clandestine churches of their own. For example, Thomas Holcroft, who had been ejected from Great Gransden, founded an Independent chapel. The oldest dissenting churches in the county were already established: these were the Baptist chapels at Fenstanton and Warboys, founded in 1644. Both these congregations were strongly influenced by Henry Denne, a parliamentary soldier who commenced his preaching ministry in Huntingdonshire during the early 1640s. There were close links between the two congregations. An elder from Fenstanton was usually asked to ordain the elders and deacons at Warboys, and Fenstanton would usually be appealed to when disputes arose in its sister congregation. Indeed, the two chapels were actually united for several years after 1714, when 89

72   18th-century Baptist chapel at Great Gidding.

members were recorded for both churches. This figure had declined to 52 members by 1725, although the Baptist church was to enjoy a revival in Huntingdonshire later in the 18th century. These churches served a community drawn from a large region, including parts of Cambridgeshire and Bedfordshire as well as Huntingdonshire. In 1676, members of the Fenstanton congregation were living at Godmanchester, the Hemingfords and St Ives, whilst a member of the Warboys congregation in 1688 originated from Chatteris. Baptisms practised by these early churches were usually performed in the river Ouse at Earith or Needingworth.

The Quakers became established as a dissenting group during the Common-wealth era. They were heavily persecuted under both the Cromwellian and the Restoration regimes, and many of them sought refuge in the overseas settle-ments in the New World. Their leader, George Fox, visited Huntingdon in 1656 and succeeded in converting the mayor's wife to Quakerism. They became a relatively strong movement in Huntingdonshire after 1660, many local members being imprisoned in the gaol at Huntingdon. Altogether, about fifty Quakers were gaoled throughout the county in 1663. Groups of them could be found in isolated parts of Huntingdonshire: at Kings Ripton, Bluntisham, Winwick and Monks Hardwick (near St Neots) for instance. In 1676, William and Francis Throssel of Winwick were cited before the ecclesiastical courts for 'being reputed

Quakers and for refusing to come to church in tyme of divine service for the space of three months past'. Quakers were sometimes mistrusted as much by other dissenting sects as by Anglicans. The early records of the Warboys Baptist congregation has several references to members who left to become Quakers. In 1657 Judith Kitson was expelled 'for neglecting to assemble with the church, following the errors of those people called Quakers, and refusing admonition'.

Dissenting chapels could apply for licences for their chapels under the terms of the Declaration of Indulgence in 1672. No Huntingdonshire Quaker groups troubled to apply, but seven local congregations of Presbyterians, six of Independents and five of Baptists did so.

The Evangelical Revival

The late 17th century witnessed a consolidation of the early dissenting movement, but both Anglicanism and the nonconformist churches had generally reached a passive and static position by the early 18th century. The Evangelical Revival of the mid-18th century was a reaction against this period of spiritual sterility. It resulted eventually in the creation of the Methodist church, but it was originally fostered by a group of Anglicans who had passed through a conversion experience between 1735 and 1760. The most notable members of the group were the brothers John and Charles Wesley. In general, the Revival was a reaction against 18th-century rationalism, and it depended upon extensive field preaching and the leadership of a group of educated and dedicated men.

John Berridge, vicar of Everton on the Bedfordshire borders between 1755 and 1793, was one early leader of the Revival who took part in field preaching campaigns throughout Huntingdonshire and the neighbouring counties of Bedfordshire, Cambridgeshire and Hertfordshire. Huntingdonshire also benefited from the attentions of John Wesley, who first visited the county during the winter of 1774, when his journal records that he preached in a large barn at Godmanchester. Several members of his congregation at this meeting returned to establish a preaching ministry at St Neots. The first Methodist chapels in the county were built at Huntingdon in 1779, at St Ives in 1792 and at St Neots in 1794. Wesley mentioned 'the new house at Huntingdon' during a visit in 1780.

His preaching was apparently confined to the southern half of the county. He visited Huntingdon, Godmanchester, St Ives, St Neots and Buckden on several occasions between 1774 and 1788, and apparently had a special affection for the Methodists at St Neots. In December 1784 he recorded in his journal that 'I preached at St Neots to the largest congregation I ever saw here, and I know not that ever I saw them so affected; it seemed as if God had touched all their hearts'. Again, he recorded in November 1788 that 'we had a lovely congregation at St Neots who seemed ripe for the promise'. On the other hand, Methodism did not at first find such fertile soil at Huntingdon and Godmanchester. Wesley noted in 1788 that 'about noon I preached at Huntingdon and in the evening at Godmanchester. Still it is the day of small things here, but a few are still fighting the good fight of faith'.

73 *Nonconformist church at St Neots.*

74 *Methodist chapel at Huntingdon.*

The Anglican church also benefited considerably from the Evangelical Revival, as many advocates of this movement did not leave the established church. A few Huntingdonshire clergy fell into this category, including Henry Venn, rector of Yelling between 1771 and 1797. His son John founded the Church Missionary Society in 1799, another fruit of the Revival.

Very few early converts to the Revival came from the nonconformist churches, but this movement did eventually greatly influence both the Baptist and the Independent churches. The great era of chapel-building, during the late 18th century and on into the 19th century, was one result of the Revival. New nonconformist chapels, most of them Baptist, were built throughout Huntingdonshire during the late 18th century. The chapels at Great Gidding, Bluntisham, Hail Weston, Great Gransden, Kimbolton, St Ives, St Neots and Spaldwick are examples of this. Many other nonconformist chapels appeared during the 19th century.

Their locations are precisely given in the Ecclesiastical Census of 1851, the only religious census ever made in England. This shows clearly that the pattern of nonconformity in Huntingdonshire had altered dramatically since the mid-18th century. The Methodists now had the largest number of chapels, a total of 43 altogether. Of these, 31 were described as 'Wesleyan Methodist', 11 as 'Primitive Methodists' and one, at Yaxley, as 'Bible Christian'. This last was a Methodist sect that originated in North Devon in 1815, and was little known outside the south-west of England.

The Baptists had now sunk to second place in the county, although their total of 30 chapels is still an

impressive figure. The Baptists were
traditionally strong in Huntingdonshire
due to the work of Henry Denne in the
mid-17th century, and they had also
benefited greatly from the Evangelical
Revival. There were another four places
of worship, called Union chapels, which
contained members from both the Baptist and Independent churches. Besides
these Union chapels, the Independents
still had six of their own. These were
often supported by the more prosperous
members of the community. The chapel
at St Neots, for instance, was bolstered
by the attendance of James Paine, the
prosperous brewer, and his family.

Other early nonconformist sects
in Huntingdonshire, such as the
Quakers, Moravians and Unitarians,
were in decline by 1851. Several
Quaker meeting-houses, such as those
at Monks Hardwick, Midloe, Stirtloe
and Little Paxton, had closed before
the end of the 18th century. By 1851,
they had just three meeting-houses left
in the county, whilst the Moravians had
two chapels and the Unitarians a soli-
tary chapel at Kimbolton. There were
also four chapels in the county that refused to label themselves as belonging
to any recognised sect, calling themselves 'Protestant Nonconformists' or 'Calvinists'.

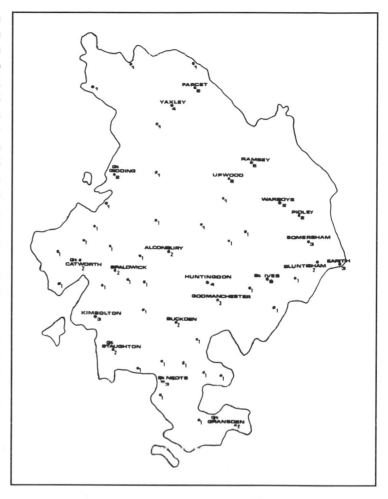

75 *Map showing the Ecclesiastical Census of 1851.*

The spread of nonconformist chapels throughout Huntingdonshire was by
no means even in 1851. The hundred of Norman Cross, in the north, had only
six parishes containing nonconformist chapels (of which there were 11 altogether),
and 17 where the inhabitants received spiritual guidance from an Anglican
incumbent alone. Nonconformist chapels appeared in far greater numbers in the
southern two-thirds of the county, as can be seen clearly on the map. The
hundred of Leightonstone had 23, that of Toseland had 24, whilst the hundred
of Hurstingstone boasted forty-one.

Parishes also differed from each other, some having several chapels whilst
others had none. St Ives, with its eight chapels, had the largest number in the
county. The buildings also varied greatly in size and in the number of seats
provided. The Bluntisham Baptist chapel contained 700 places, and the St
Neots Wesleyan Methodist chapel could seat 721 persons. At the other extreme,
the Warboys Primitive Methodists had seating for only 27, and the Little Paxton

Independent chapel was simply a room in a cottage in which 26 people could be seated.

The 19th-century Oxford Movement did not have a great impact on Huntingdonshire, at least not at this date. An Anglican clergyman, the Reverend Frederick William Faber, rector of Elton between 1843 and 1845, became a firm supporter of the Movement. He was converted to Roman Catholicism in 1845, at which point he gave up his living and moved to London, where he founded the Roman Catholic Oratory at Brompton.

The Salvation Army is one of the most recent nonconformist sects to arrive in Huntingdonshire. They first appeared at St Neots in 1883, and a Citadel was opened there in 1891. The Army's meeting rooms at Godmanchester date to 1887. The sect did not at first inspire the respect which it now engenders. Like the early Methodists, they had to endure a great deal of public heckling and violent behaviour. The *Hunts Post* noted in November 1887 that a Salvation Army band playing in Huntingdon had been treated to a barrage of coarse songs and rotten eggs. At St Neots in 1883, they were accused by the magistrates of 'thrusting their religious views upon the public in an ostentatious manner'.

13

Huntingdonshire Schools

Education in Huntingdonshire was provided on a piecemeal basis prior to the reforms of the 19th century. Medieval schools were not unknown, but elementary education only became fairly widespread from the 16th century onwards. Ramsey Abbey maintained a school within its precincts; a 12th-century charter records the presence of a school at Huntingdon run by St Mary's Priory; and a school had appeared at Godmanchester by the 14th century.

Elementary Schools

Village schools are first recorded from the 16th century onwards, often as temporary institutions dependent upon a single educated individual, usually the local clergyman. Leland records a 'fre schole' at Leighton Bromswold in the 1530s, run by 'Smithe now incumbent'. Other early schools appeared at Buckden in 1661, Farcet in 1673 and at Great Gransden around 1670. The first comprehensive list of schools still surviving for Huntingdonshire is the list of charity schools to be found in Cox's *History of Huntingdonshire*, written in 1730. It names 18 schools, a reasonably high figure for a small county like Huntingdonshire. The much larger county of Devon, for example, contained only 25 charity schools in 1724.

The charity school movement was sponsored by the Society for the Promotion of Christian Knowledge after 1699, but it still depended almost exclusively upon the philanthropy of local landowners and other wealthy patrons. Most of the charity schools in Huntingdonshire were relatively small, catering for numbers between the 60 pupils taught at Stanground down to the four at Folksworth. The pupils at Glatton and Holme were especially fortunate, being provided with clothes as well as with a basic education. Early charity schools, however, were usually dependent upon endowments made in an individual's will. Sometimes this led to a prolonged legal battle when a relative contested the will, so delaying the establishment of a school for several years.

The supervision of elementary education in England in the early 19th century was largely in the hands of two voluntary societies. The first of these was the National Society for Promoting the Education of the Poor in the Principles of the Established Church (founded in 1811), which assisted schools run by the Church of England. The British and Foreign Bible Society, founded in 1808, acted on a non-denominational basis, but in practice mainly aided non-

76 *Former grammar school at Huntingdon, now the Cromwell Museum.*

conformist schools. For this reason, Church of England schools are usually described in records as 'National' schools, whilst others are known as 'British' schools. For instance, the Wesleyan, Baptist and Independent churches in St Neots came together in 1844 to found a British school in the town.

State intervention in education began in 1833, when the government gave these two societies grants. The Education Act of 1870 led to the appearance of school boards elected by ratepayers, which were to establish schools in areas previously poorly supplied. These institutions became known as 'board schools'. Education finally became compulsory in 1876, and free schooling universally available in 1891.

Further information on the elementary schools of Huntingdonshire can be found in the county directories of the late 19th century. *Kelly's Directory of Huntingdonshire* for 1877 shows that there were then 52 National schools in the county, only seven British schools, and 33 which were variously described, as 'endowed', 'parochial' or just simply 'school'. There were only nine board schools at this date, some seven years after the establishment of school boards. These 'deprived' areas which had required state intervention were Covington, Grafham, Woodhurst, Offord Cluny, Offord Darcy, Sawtry, Stibbington, Little Stukeley and Yelling.

This picture had altered considerably by 1898, according to the *Kelly's Directory* for that year. There were now 25 board schools, several appearing in the towns for the first time. These new board schools were at Brampton (two), Colne, Godmanchester, Hartford, Hemingford Grey (two), Houghton, Kimbolton, St Ives (three), Somersham, Spaldwick, Great Staughton and Warboys. The number of National schools had hardly changed (51), but there were now only two British schools. This was because several described under this heading in 1877 had now become board schools. The directory also shows that there were still 20 villages where children had to go elsewhere for schooling. For instance, children from Toseland had to attend the school at Yelling, while pupils from Easton and Stow Longa went to Spaldwick. The walk to school at that date must have been very wearisome, and the temptation to miss school was sometimes too great, especially when casual employment was available. The schoolchildren of Huntingdonshire played truant for many reasons, including fruit-picking, lace-making and bird-scaring.

The school boards were abolished in 1902, and the supervision of elementary education was taken over by the new county councils. The depopulation of rural areas since 1945 has led to the closure of at least twenty elementary schools, although a few new ones have appeared as well, at Stanground, Godmanchester, Orton Longueville, Upwood and St Neots.

Grammar Schools and Secondary Education

Grammar schools were established in several Huntingdonshire towns during the 16th and 17th centuries. A master at such a school was licensed to teach either reading or writing, or Latin grammar—hence the name 'grammar' school. Four such schools were founded at Huntingdon, Godmanchester, Ramsey and Kimbolton. The 'free school' at Huntingdon was founded in 1565. This former medieval hospital had two levels, the upper chamber being the schoolmaster's living accommodation, and the lower the schoolroom. The schoolmaster had the aid of a writing-master and a classical assistant by the 19th century. Originally the school was intended for the sons of Huntingdon freemen, who were taught free of charge, and the offspring of local gentry, who paid fees.

The school was no longer attracting pupils from these backgrounds by the 19th century. At its peak, it had taught about seventy to eighty boys, about half of whom were boarders. There were less than forty pupils by 1818, however, and by 1867 numbers had fallen still further to 10 boarders and seven day-boys. The school was reorganised under a board of governors in 1895. By 1905 it had become a mixed secondary school. New premises were opened in 1939, and the old building was vacated. The school became comprehensive in 1970 when it moved to its present position in and around Hinchingbrooke House, the former home of the earls of Sandwich. The distinctive green uniform worn by the pupils originates from the amalgamation (in 1895) between the Free School and Walden's charity school. The latter had opened in 1719, and a later bequest to it had resulted in the pupils wearing green coats. The school thus became known as the Green Coat School and brought this tradition to the amalgamation.

The brick building which housed the grammar school at Godmanchester can still be seen. Letters Patent for a free grammar school in the town were issued by Queen Elizabeth I in 1561, hence the inscription *Eliz. Reg. Hujus Scholae Fundatrix* that can still be seen over the door. The school had degenerated to the level of an elementary school by the early 19th century, although there were still about eighty pupils there in 1864.

The grammar school at Kimbolton was founded in 1600 and was originally situated between the church and the road passing through the town. These early buildings were demolished in 1874. In 1827, there were 30 boarders, 30 free-scholars and 16 fee-paying day-boys at the school. By 1924, numbers had risen to 100 boarders and 55 day boys. The school is now housed within Kimbolton Castle, the former mansion of the dukes of Manchester, and is run as a mixed private school.

77 Kimbolton Castle, now a school.

The grammar school at Ramsey dates from a grant made by the Cromwell family in 1652 of 120 acres of drained fen land, the income from which was to provide for a school. This establishment was rebuilt in 1791, by which time there were some eighty boys there. By 1866, it was only attracting the children of the poorer inhabitants of Ramsey, but its re-establishment as a secondary school in that year led to its revival. By 1926 it had become co-educational, and in 1937 it moved to Ramsey Abbey, the former home of the Fellowes family. By 1972 it had become a comprehensive school.

The most modern grammar school in Huntingdonshire was that at Orton Longueville, founded in 1959. It occupies Orton Longueville Hall, the former home of the marquess of Huntly, and is now run as a comprehensive school.

The Education Act of 1944 introduced secondary education on a universal basis. Increased demand for advanced schooling has led to new secondary schools being opened at Huntingdon, St Ives, St Neots, Ramsey, Sawtry and Stanground. St Peter's School in Huntingdon, a former secondary modern school, was re-organised on a comprehensive basis in 1970, as was the St Ivo school at St Ives. Longsands School at St Neots was founded in 1960, and had become comprehensive by 1966. The Ailwyn Community School at Ramsey, a former secondary modern, now functions as a lower school for the Abbey School. The Ernulf comprehensive school was opened in St Neots as recently as 1971. Other avenues of further education exist at Huntingdon Technical College and its wing at St Neots, and at the Sawtry Village College.

14

Agriculture in the 19th Century

Parliamentary Enclosure, 1760-1869

The century between 1750 and 1850 is generally viewed as the era of enclosure by Act of parliament, when the land in the remaining English open-field parishes was enclosed and divided among the parish landowners. A General Enclosure Act was passed through parliament in 1750, and thereafter landowners either used this Act, or sent their own private bill through parliament.

Huntingdonshire was part of the wet clayland belt of the Midlands, where enclosure had long been postponed. Enclosure was an expensive business, and this was the main reason for the delay, especially when the land involved was believed to be poor and infertile. Landowners favouring enclosure had to hold over half of the agricultural land in a parish before a bill could be sent through parliament. This posed no problem where the lord of the manor favoured enclosure, and where there were few freehold farmers living in the parish. The bill of enclosure was then drawn up, and a committee formed to hear the arguments for and against enclosure. Commissioners were sent out to survey the parish, check claims and draw up a large map showing land ownership. These maps are often valuable sources for discovering the appearance of open-field parishes before enclosure.

Upon the passing of the enclosure act, field boundaries were marked out over the former open-fields, hedges were planted and ditches dug, and new straight roads with wide verges were laid out. It was scarcely surprising that the costs of enclosure were sometimes the last nail in the coffin for peasant farmers, who were then obliged to sell up and seek work elsewhere.

Most Huntingdonshire parishes retained their open-fields until the era of parliamentary enclosure. Arthur Young recorded in the 1770s that the landscape between St Neots and Kimbolton was generally open, whilst Thomas Stone, writing in 1793, estimated that the county contained 130,000 acres of open-fields and commonland to 66,000 acres of enclosed arable, pasture and woodland. This did not include a further 44,000 acres of Fenland. George Maxwell, also writing in 1793, believed that about half of the upland parishes of Huntingdonshire were still unenclosed at this date, and that only 41 out of 106 parishes in the county were wholly enclosed. This picture had changed considerably by 1811 when Parkinson wrote his study of Huntingdonshire. He stated that 'more than two-thirds of the county are enclosed'. He also made a detailed

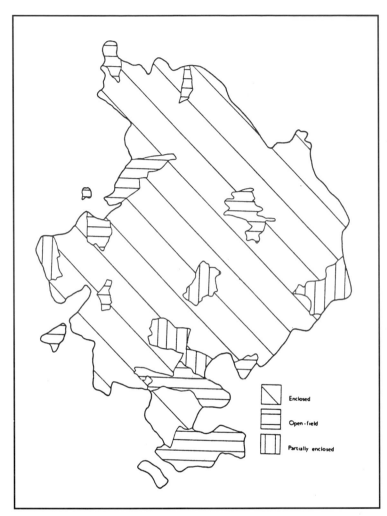

78 Map showing Huntingdonshire parishes with open and enclosed fields c.1811.

analysis of each parish, from which it would appear that only 19 parishes were still in their open-field state, while six others were partially enclosed. The remainder were almost wholly enclosed, including Orton Waterville, Stilton and Great Staughton, which were 'enclosing this year'.

Enclosure often depended on the presence of a determined landlord, who was prepared to enforce his will on his tenants. One example was Sir Robert Bernard (1739-89) of Brampton Hall. He was one of the principal landowners in the parishes of Brampton, Houghton, Wyton, Little Stukeley, Hartford, Easton, Spaldwick, Ellington and Grafham, and he was able to bring about the enclosure of all of these parishes between 1772 and 1776.

Altogether, 74 different enclosure acts affecting Huntingdonshire parishes were passed through parliament between 1760 and 1869, but 12 of them involved the enclosure of less than 1,000 acres. Several parishes affected by parliamentary enclosure therefore already contained areas of enclosed land.

The last manor in Huntingdonshire to be enclosed was Great Gidding. The three open-fields in this parish were enclosed in 1858, and the commonland in 1869. It is not easy to discover why the process was so long delayed here. The lord of the manor was Earl Fitzwilliam, head of a family from Milton Park near Peterborough, and he had no special reason for postponing enclosure. One reason for the delay was probably the presence of a small group of freehold farmers in the village. Earl Fitzwilliam may also have not wanted to antagonise his copyhold tenants on the manor, many of whom also held parcels of freehold land.

Some of the effects of enclosure can be studied in the case of Great Gidding, with the aid of the censuses dating between 1851 and 1871, and of the transfers of copyhold tenancies listed in the manor court records. There were usually about three or four copyhold transfers a year. These transfers increased in number to a total of 11 in 1859 and to 27 in 1870, the two years following the enclosures of the open-fields and of the commonland. The early censuses show that Great Gidding usually supported only one or two families described

79 *Old bridge and 19th-century mill at Huntingdon.*

as paupers, but in 1871 there were 11 such families. It would appear that the enclosure of the commonland had a more devastating effect on the village community than that of the open-fields. The peasant farmers were probably able to survive the latter, but really suffered when they lost their former access to the commonland. This meant that they had now lost the vital areas of rough pasture where they had previously grazed a few cows and other livestock. After 1869 their entire livelihood had to come from their few acres of enclosed land. The agricultural depression after 1870 added to the effects of this last enclosure, resulting in the transfer of these small farms to the larger village landowners. The former peasant farmers either left the village or became farm labourers. Their frustrations are echoed by John Clare, the Northamptonshire poet who himself came from peasant stock:

> Enclosure came, and trampled on the grave
> Of labour's rights, and left the poor a slave.

However, enclosure should not be seen as the only reason for the disappearance of the small-scale farmer in Huntingdonshire. The decline in their numbers had been progressing since the 17th century, and parliamentary enclosure merely increased the burdens on those who remained. On the other hand, the survival of many open-field manors until a relatively late date probably delayed their final extinction. Parkinson stated in 1811 that the old enclosed areas of the county were 'generally speaking in the hands of large proprietors; the property in the new enclosures and open fields much diffused'. Despite this, there was a large number of small landowners remaining in the county at the time of the 1873 Return of Owners of Land. This source gives a total of 1,816 landowners who held less than one acre in Huntingdonshire, with another 1,619 who held between one and 50 acres. This figure does not, of course, include tenant farmers. The owners of less than one acre must have been mainly householders following non-agricultural trades, but many of the holders of under 50

The 1873 Return of Owners of Land	
Amount of land	**Numbers of landowners**
Under one acre	1,816
One-50 acres	1,619
50-100 acres	150
100-200 acres	134
200-300 acres	75
300-400 acres	33
400-500 acres	16
500-600 acres	15
600-700 acres	9
700-800 acres	4
800-900 acres	5
900-1000 acres	5
Over 1000 acres	36

Landowners of over 1,000 acres:

1. Edward Fellowes of Ramsey Abbey, Hunts. 15,629
2. Duke of Manchester of Kimbolton Castle, Hunts. 13,835
3. John M. Heathcote of Conington Castle, Hunts. 7,144
4. William Wells of Holme, Hunts. 5,792
5. Marquis of Huntley of Cotterstock Hall 5,711
6. Hon. G. W. Fitzwilliam of Milton Hall, Peterborough 5,202
7. Cambridge University colleges 4,223
8. Lord Chesham of Latimer 3,787
9. Earl of Carysfort of Elton Hall, Hunts. 3,654
10. Anglican Ecclesiastical Commissioners 3,559
11. Hon. Colonel Dunscombe of Waresley Park, Hunts. 3,407
12. W. Duberley of Great Staughton, Hunts. 3,224
13. Earl of Sandwich of Hinchingbrooke House, Hunts. 3,219
14. G.O. Newton of Croxton Park 3,209
15. Richard H. Hussey of Upwood, Hunts. 3,135
16. Sir Henry Pelly of London 2,718
17. Lord Saye and Sele of Banby 2,461
18. George Thornhill of Diddington, Hunts. 2,372
19. Charles Robertson of Washingley Hall 2,128
20. A.H. Smith-Barry of Northwick 2,079
21. John R. Mills of Tunbridge Wells 1,891
22. Theodore Webb of Great Gransden, Hunts. 1,837
23. Lord Overstone of Northamptonshire 1,712
24. G.W. Rowley of St Neots, Hunts. 1,629
25. Edward Reynolds of Little Paxton, Hunts. 1,605
26. J.R. Welstead of Kimbolton, Hunts. 1,522
27. Francis Pym of Sandy, Bedfordshire 1,492
28. Duke of Bedford of Woburn Abbey 1,334
29. James Rust of Alconbury, Hunts. 1,273
30. Bishop of Peterborough 1,246
31. Charles de la Pryme of Westow 1,228
32. Rev. L.R. Brown of Suffolk 1,091
33. Railway companies 1,075
34. Duke of Buccleuch of London 1,065
35. Crown property 1,055
36. L.J. Torkington of Tunbridge Wells 1,012

acres were probably small-scale farmers. The numbers of landowners in 1873 **80** *19th-century mill on*
holding more than a hundred acres decreases sharply, as the tables demonstrate. *the river Ouse at St Ives.*
The names of the 36 landowners who held more than a thousand acres within
the county are given on the tables.

19th-century Labourers

Agricultural labourers during this period were sometimes affected by enclosure,
if it meant that they lost access to commonland where they had formerly grazed
livestock. The life of the rural labourer in the 19th century was invariably hard
and bitter. He might be employed by a charitable farmer who would help him
during lean times, but he usually had to live in a small and squalid cottage, was
hired by the day and given nothing if rain and snow halted work. The sole
protection against starvation was the workhouse.

   An account of the life of the labourers of Huntingdonshire in 1793 was
given by George Maxwell. He wrote that 'the poor in general have dwellings
suited to their station; and as almost every one of them may grow his own
potatoes, and have constant employment if he pleases, they are generally as
little disposed to emigrate from Huntingdonshire'. This optimistic picture was
slightly contradicted by Thomas Stone, writing during the same year. He declared
that Huntingdonshire labourers tended to migrate to other counties in search of
work in the summer, and the labour required by local farmers had to be provided by the 'accidental peregrinations of the Irish'.

Sacred

TO THE MEMORY OF

THOMAS GARNER

who died Sept 30ᵗʰ 1826.

Aged 77 Years.

My sledge and hammers lie declined,
My bellows too have lost their . wind
My fires extinct my forge decayed.
My vice is in the dust all laid,
My coal is spent, my iron gone
My nails are drove, my work is done
My fire dried corpse here lies at rest,
My soul smoke like soars to be blest
ALSO
CATHERINE who died 7ᵗʰ July 1833

Aged 63 Years
Also two of his children
rest near this place

81 *Blacksmith's grave-stone at Houghton.*

The practice of employing Irish labourers continued during the 19th century, as farmers used them as cheap labour which could not become a burden on the parish. Naturally this led to great resentment from the local farmworkers, who saw their employment prospects threatened. Disturbances and riots broke out in St Ives in 1831 over this issue, and again at Old Hurst and Woodhurst in 1840, at Godmanchester in 1842, and at Orton Waterville in 1853.

In 1811 Parkinson gave an interesting account of the diet of the Huntingdonshire labourer. He wrote that 'pork and dumplings, or puddings or potatoes, are the food of three-fourths of the parishes; with milk pottage, or milk and bread for breakfast, and in the harvest in many of these they are allowed mutton, beef, etc'.

Many labourers had to walk long distances before they even started work, because of the 'open' and 'closed' parish system. Landowners could destroy cottages in certain parishes, to prevent labourers becoming a burden on the Poor Rate, should they fall on hard times. These labourers and their families were then obliged to live in 'open' parishes, often the local market town. About a quarter of the parishes of Huntingdonshire were reported as 'closed' in the early 19th century. The problem was more acute in other areas, such as the north Midlands and East Yorkshire, where about 40 per cent of parishes were classified as 'closed'.

Times of severe hardship sometimes led to rioting in rural areas of Huntingdonshire, as in 1816, and during 1830 and 1831. Enquiries into these riots put the causes down as fear of new agricultural machinery, which might put men out of work; poor wages; and general worries about unemployment. For example, the rioting which occurred in the north-west of Huntingdonshire during November and December 1830 was provoked by the new threshing machines owned by local farmers. Machines were destroyed on the farms of

William Wright of Upton, William Cheney of Hamerton, John and Christmas Bullen of Buckworth, Joseph Briggs of Old Weston and John Hatfield of Sawtry. These riots saw the invocation of 'Captain Swing', a symbolic leader, whose name was used to sign the threatening letters sent to farmers in an effort to persuade them to get rid of the hated machines. Most of the labourers involved were given short prison terms or even acquitted, but two of them, William Horner and William Hughes, were sentenced to seven years' transportation. Their descendants are probably still living in Australia.

Huntingdonshire labourers were transported for other offences apart from rioting. William Boddington and Thomas Grant (who again originated from the rural area west of Sawtry) were both transported in 1829 for the theft of a sheep. In 1837 Hayes Savage and William Quincey of Old Weston were transported for 10 years for the same offence. At their trial, Savage claimed that 'great poverty was the only cause of my having stolen this sheep'.

By the end of the 19th century, labourers in Huntingdonshire, as elsewhere, were starting to use another weapon apart from riots in their quest for improved working conditions. The *Hunts Post* recorded several farm-workers' strikes at this time. In 1907 there was a brief strike at Hamerton, and another one, involving some fifty to sixty men, occurred in 1914 at Great Catworth.

Rural Changes in the Late 19th Century

The long-term effects of parliamentary enclosure, together with the agricultural depression of the 1870s, led to a marked depopulation in the upland clay areas of Huntingdonshire during the late 19th century. Only the urban population, as well as that of the Fenland and the brick-field areas of Fletton, Yaxley and Warboys increased. Some villages in the clayland areas, such as Steeple Gidding, virtually disappeared from the map by the 20th century.

The population increase in the Huntingdonshire fens was partly caused by the labour demands of the expanding brick industry, but it was also caused by the final assault upon the Fenland marshes. This drainage programme resulted in the disappearance of the meres of Whittlesey, Ramsey and Ugg. The coming of the railways during the mid-19th century also benefited the

82 *Water pump at St Ives.*

Fenland area by promoting the viability of arable over livestock farming. Crops such as potatoes, sugar-beet and garden vegetables could now be grown on the rich Fenland soils, to be rapidly transported to the London markets by rail. New cottages were built alongside the long straight roads that had been constructed over the Fenland. The Church of England had now apparently learnt the lesson of the past, that nonconformity flourished in large parishes, where people living on the parish boundaries could remain free from the social pressure of squire and parson. In the 1860s two new parishes were made out of the single large parish of Ramsey, and new churches were built, Ramsey St Mary and St Thomas's at Pondersbridge. Another new parish, around the village of Holme, was created out of the parish of Glatton in 1857. The nonconformists likewise created new chapels in the fens.

A new form of agriculture that appeared in Huntingdonshire at this time was almost certainly another result of the coming of the railways. This was the appearance of fruit orchards at Colne and neighbouring parishes, which were first planted between 1860 and 1880. *Kelly's Directory of Huntingdonshire* for 1869 states that at Colne 'the principal crops are wheat and beans', but by 1877 this phrase had been altered to 'the principal crops are corn and fruit'. Also in 1877, Thomas Essom of Colne appeared in the *Directory* as a 'farmer and fruit salesman'. During the 1870s, growers at Somersham started transporting greengages, cherries and plums to the north of England. Men from Earith at the same date were selling gooseberries, blackcurrants, plums and apples. The later Huntingdonshire directories show the expansion of this industry. In 1890 two fruit salesmen and one fruit grower were recorded at Colne but, by 1910, 11 fruit growers and one fruit salesman were named. This contrasts with pre-1877 entries for the parish, when only farmers and market gardeners were recorded.

15

Railways, Reform and Redcoats

The Age of the Railways

The event which most clearly marked the arrival of the modern era in Huntingdonshire was the incorporation of the county within the national railway network during the mid-19th century. The Great Northern line which passed from north to south through the county was opened in 1850. The laying of the track over the peat fen north of Abbots Ripton was a major feat of engineering. The embankment crossing the Fenland had to be constructed on alternate layers of faggots and peat, sunk into the soft ground in order to force out the water.

The Great Northern line was not, however, the first length of track to be opened in the county. The earliest line was constructed before 1845, to run between Peterborough and Blisworth, passing through Stibbington and the two Ortons. A station built in barnack stone, lying near Stibbington but called

83 *Huntingdon railway bridge, now demolished.*

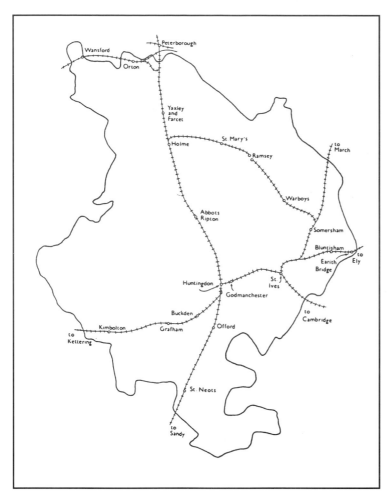

84 *Map showing the railways of Huntingdonshire.*

Wansford Station, is now the centre of the Nene Valley Railway, which has preserved the length of track between Wansford and Peterborough. Another branch line appeared during the 1860s, running between Huntingdon and Kettering, with stations at Buckden, Grafham and Kimbolton. A line between Godmanchester and St Ives was built in 1847 to link up with the Cambridge to St Ives line. Unfortunately, the connecting line between Godmanchester and the present station at Huntingdon was not constructed until 1875. Before that date, passengers had to travel by coach or carrier between the two stations. Another branch line between St Ives and Wisbech, with a station at Somersham, was opened in 1848. The branch between Holme and Ramsey opened in 1864, between St Ives and Ely in 1878, and between Ramsey and Somersham in 1889.

Huntingdon did not benefit from the coming of the railways as greatly as, for instance, Peterborough. Indeed, by rendering long-distance coach travel uneconomic, the railways enforced decline on Huntingdon and other coaching centres in the county. The railways also ensured the collapse by the early 20th century of the river trade on the Ouse, especially the transportation of coal. However, other industries were able to develop as a result of the arrival of the railways, for instance fruit growing in the Fenland region, as noted in the previous chapter. Other Huntingdonshire farmers used rail to transport milk and butter to London. Livestock farmers started sending cattle by train, when it was realised that animals could arrive far more quickly, and in much better condition, than if they travelled by hoof.

Brick-making was a crucial industry which developed because of the better facilities for long-distance transportation provided by the railways. Patches of brick-clay exist near many of the villages bordering the fens, and there are very large deposits at Fletton and Yaxley. The brick industry had already become firmly established by the early 19th century, but its fortunes were dramatically boosted by the arrival of the railways. The first brick-works at Fletton opened in 1879, and the village's population increased from just under two hundred inhabitants in 1831 to almost two thousand by 1881. A brick-works opened at

85 *Steam trains near Buckden in the 1950s.*

Huntingdon in 1886, but closed when it could not compete with Fletton. The Warboys brick-works opened in 1895, and is still in operation.

The dangers, as well as the benefits, of the new form of transportation were demonstrated in Huntingdonshire on 22 January 1876, when Abbots Ripton was the scene of a famous train disaster. A coal train being shunted into sidings was hit by the Scottish express, which itself was in collision with the London train coming from the other direction. Fifteen people were killed, and Huntingdon was in mourning for the following four days. This disaster led to radical changes in signalling methods throughout the United Kingdom rail network.

The revenge of road transport upon the railways was not long in coming. The modern motor-car, using virtually the same routes as the old 19th-century horse-drawn coaches, has brought about the decline of the railways. Only the former Great Northern line between London and York is still used by British Rail, and all the branch lines except for the Peterborough to Wansford stretch have now disappeared. All these lines were closed between 1958 and 1970, the last one to go being the St Ives to Cambridge section. It is often difficult even to trace the course of these old branch lines, as many embankments have been levelled. It is fitting that the increased traffic on the roads has saved many of the old Huntingdonshire coaching inns from the oblivion into which they fell, bringing them new customers and prosperity.

Administrative Reforms

The 19th century saw the reform of local government, for so long the preserve of the J.P.s and parish officials. St Ives gained borough status at last in 1874,

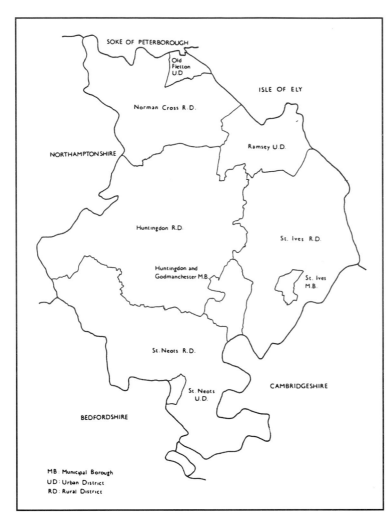

86 *Map showing local government districts within Huntingdonshire in 1961.*

while St Neots was placed under the control of a body of town commissioners in 1816. Both systems replaced the rule of the lord of the manor, the Duke of Manchester in the case of St Ives and the Earl of Sandwich at St Neots. The town commissioners of St Neots were replaced by an elected local board in 1876 and finally by an urban district council in 1894.

The poor law was reformed in 1834, placing parishes into 'unions' controlled by boards of guardians, each union maintaining a workhouse. This was another erosion of the power of the J.P., as was the introduction of elected county councils in 1888. J.P.s were left solely with responsibility for law and order, but the local gentry still kept a good deal of their old influence. Many stood for election to the county councils and soon dominated these new institutions. County council territories were divided in 1894 into urban districts, rural districts and parish councils. Huntingdonshire was divided into four rural districts, Norman Cross, Huntingdon, St Ives and St Neots. There were also three municipal boroughs at Huntingdon, Godmanchester and St Ives, and three urban districts at Fletton, St Neots, and Ramsey. The appearance of Fletton as an urban district was of course the result of its expansion during the late 19th century.

County police forces were gradually introduced after 1835, although they did not become compulsory until 1856. The Huntingdonshire constabulary, which was formed in 1857, was therefore a late development of this kind. A new gaol was built at St Ives in 1842, and a new county prison at Huntingdon replaced the old county gaol in 1830. Huntingdon finally lost its prison to Bedford in 1892.

Military Matters

Huntingdonshire was little affected by wars after 1660, although the Jacobite invasion of northern England in 1745 led to funds being raised by the inhabitants of Huntingdon for the use of the anti-Jacobite forces. A prisoner-of-war camp was constructed at Norman Cross during the Napoleonic Wars, and was

XI *Houghton Mill.*

XII *Portrait of Oliver Cromwell.*

XIII *Ramsey Drain near Ramsey St Mary's.*

XIV *Barograph at Bluntisham.*

occupied by French and Dutch soldiers and sailors between 1797 and 1816. Norman Cross was one of three English prisons—Dartmoor being another—which were built for this purpose. About ten thousand men were imprisoned there during the war, having arrived after a journey by Fenland waterways to Peterborough or Yaxley. Several thousand English militiamen were stationed there at one time to guard the prisoners. The presence of so many men in northern Huntingdonshire must have had a great effect upon the economy and social structure of the area. The governor's house still stands at Norman Cross, and there is a monument by the side of the A1 marking the site of the French cemetery, where about one thousand seven hundred prisoners were buried. Peterborough Museum and the Norris Museum at St Ives both have fine displays of ships and other items carved from animal bones by the prisoners and sold to local people.

87 *Model of ship made from animal bones by French prisoners of war at Norman Cross between 1797 and 1814, now in the Norris Museum at St Ives.*

One local man spent most of the Napoleonic Wars as a prisoner of the French. John Hopkinson of Little Gidding was in the navy when he was captured in 1804. He was imprisoned at Verdun until 1814, before returning to Huntingdonshire to end his days as rector of Alwalton in the north of the county. No doubt several local men made names for themselves during the wars; one of them who did so was Granville Proby of Elton Hall. He was present at the battles of the Nile and Trafalgar, and ended his career as an admiral. He became the 3rd Earl of Carysfort in 1855, upon the death of his brother John.

The 31st Regiment of Foot became known as the Huntingdonshire Regiment after 1782. There is no record that this unit was ever stationed within the county, but several recruits came from Huntingdonshire. John Dawson and John White of Upton, for instance, joined the 31st Foot in 1824 and served in India and Afghanistan. The regiment lost its identification with Huntingdonshire in 1881, when it became known as the First Battalion the East Surrey Regiment. The colours of the 31st Foot, presented in 1848, now hang in the church of Huntingdon St Mary, where a regimental memorial to men lost during the Crimean War can also be seen. The regiment had earlier taken part in the Peninsular campaign under Wellington, where it played a significant part in the battle of Talavera, and in the campaigns of Afghanistan and China as well as the Crimea. A display of Peninsular War medals won by the regiment can now be seen in the Norris Museum.

16

The 20th Century

New Economic Developments

Agriculture in Huntingdonshire took some time to recover from the agricultural depression of the late 19th century; with Essex, the county is reputed to be one of the two counties most devastated by this period of rural decline. There was a revival during the First World War, but another slump ensued during the inter-war years, with many areas reverting back to permanent pasture.

The Smallholdings and Allotments Act of 1908 was one attempt to aid local agriculture, as well as to benefit farm labourers who wanted to establish their own farms. The Huntingdonshire County Council had by 1909 acquired an estate of 2,500 acres (10,000 acres by 1963) which was divided into units of roughly thirty-five acres. These smallholdings were generally located on the highly productive Fenland soils. About twenty new tenants a year were being installed on their own farms during the 1960s.

The Agricultural Returns of 1938 show that 90,232 acres out of the county total of 233,221 acres of land were then described as permanent pasture and rough grazing. Another 6,585 were under clover and rotation grasses, making a total of 96,817 acres of grassland in the county. The acreage under crops amounted to 95,581 acres, not including a further 9,582 acres of bare fallow. Therefore, the proportion of arable to pasture in the county in 1938 was about even. After 1940, the proportion of arable land greatly increased, owing to the demands of the war and the introduction of new machinery. It is believed by some that Huntingdonshire now possesses more arable land than at any date since the 13th century.

Kelly's Directory for 1940 lists the county's industries as being brick and tile making, paper making, parchment making, brewing, currying and tanning, iron founding, lace-making and printing. However, the last war and the period following it witnessed as great a change in industry as it did in agriculture. The county handbook of 1963 referred to new industries such as light engineering, electronics, plastics and specialised paper products. Agricultural industries included food canning at Fletton and Huntingdon, sugar processing from sugar-beet at Woodstone, mechanical tools, and a chicory factory at St Ives. The extraction of gravel and sand from the Ouse and Nene valleys has also become an important 20th-century concern. This industry first appeared during the inter-war years, with the development of concrete manufacture. Production was greatly boosted during the last war because of the construction of a large number of

88 *Late 19th-century photograph of carrier's van at Glatton.*

airfields throughout East Anglia. Demand since 1945 has been sustained by the road-building programmes of post-war governments.

The brick-works of Huntingdonshire, which developed as an important industry during the 19th century, endured a period of slump during the early 20th century. The *Hunts Post* published an article in 1905 on the acute depression in the Fletton brick-works at that time. Another article appeared in the same newspaper in 1922, again referring to the slump at Fletton. However, this industry had a revival after the last war, and about 600 million bricks per annum were being produced at Fletton during the 1960s. Brick production at Warboys has followed a similar course during the 20th century.

Car ownership, at first confined to the wealthy, has increased rapidly during the course of the century. The *Hunts Post* reported as early as 1906 the summoning of eight motorists at the Huntingdon court for driving offences at Alconbury Weston. By 1912, the firm of Windovers Ltd. of Huntingdon was advertising Panhards, Wolseleys, Daimlers and Minervas for hire, and in 1913, the Huntingdon motor business of Maddox, Murkett Brothers and Windovers were exhibiting at the Olympia Motor Show. In 1971, about 70 per cent of Huntingdonshire households possessed at least one car. The increased use of motorised transport has led to major developments in the road network of Huntingdonshire. The entire length of the A1 as it passes through the county is now dual carriageway, and by-passes round villages on its route, such as Stilton and Buckden, have been constructed. Traffic which formerly crossed the old medieval bridges at Huntingdon and St Ives has also been diverted along by-pass routes, while the A604 between Huntingdon and Cambridge has been widened and greatly improved within recent years.

In 1940 *Kelly's Directory* recorded that the inhabitants of the county were poorly supplied with water owing to a lack of springs. At that date many people were still dependent on ponds and wells. The production of a clean water supply has therefore been an important priority during recent years. The Anglian Water Authority now draws water from an artificial reservoir which was excavated near Grafham between 1962 and 1965. The surface area of Grafham Water, as it is known, is about two and a half square miles, and its circumference amounts to about ten miles. It is one of the largest lakes in England, and has taken over the former role of Whittlesey Mere for water sports, including sailing and fishing. The development of boating holidays on the Ouse and the Nene in recent years makes a significant economic impact on the county during summer months. Altogether, the introduction of modern sanitation, and electricity as well as mains water has greatly improved the quality of life within Huntingdonshire.

The 20th century has also witnessed the welcome demise of the workhouse system. The able-bodied poor during earlier centuries probably found the workhouse an unattractive but endurable haven during short periods of unemployment, but the practice of splitting families into males and females must have led to much unhappiness for those confined for longer periods. In particular, the separation of old people after a lifetime of marriage led to many early deaths. Homes for the elderly operated on a more civilised basis are now located within Huntingdonshire at Godmanchester, Stanground, Huntingdon, Yaxley, St Ives, St Neots and Ramsey.

89 *Harvest scene c.1910 on Mr. Bullimore's farm at Great Gidding.*

90 *Chinese bridge at Godmanchester.*

The Town Development Act of 1952, which aimed at reducing overcrowding in London, has led to the rapid growth of the towns of Huntingdon, St Ives and St Neots in recent years. In 1931, the population of Huntingdon stood at 4,106 people; by 1982 it had risen to 14,530 inhabitants. The populations of St Ives and St Neots have risen from 2,664 and 4,314 respectively in 1931, to 12,840 and 12,600 in 1982. The figure for St Neots would rise to 21,660 if its suburbs of Eaton Socon and Eaton Ford were included. Several villages throughout the county, particularly in the Ouse valley, have also witnessed considerable increases in their population following their development as commuter centres. Brampton, Buckden, the Hemingfords and Little Paxton now contain populations not far short of that of Huntingdon in 1931.

A few fen-edge villages (such as Sawtry and Somersham) have also expanded during recent decades, but many upland villages have found little relief from the earlier trend towards depopulation. Only two or three houses and a disused church remain at Steeple Gidding, while Anglican ministers who supervise the affairs of five or more parishes, where previously most villages boasted a resident clergyman, are becoming common. A dwindling population and improved communications have also led to the closure of many village schools, pubs and shops, leading to difficulties for those without their own means of transport.

The Two World Wars

There were several avenues open to Huntingdonshire men before the First World War if they wished to undertake part-time military service. In 1885 the *Hunts*

91 *Second World War pill-box near Ramsey.*

Post mentioned men from St Ives and Huntingdon who belonged to the 1st Cambridgeshire Rifle Volunteer Corps. There was also the Bedfordshire Imperial Yeomanry, which had a unit incorporated within it known as the Hunts Squadron. This unit was first formed at St Neots in 1902.

There were thus several part-time units containing Huntingdonshire men which were ready to be thrown into battle as soon as hostilities commenced in 1914. The Hunts Territorials were mobilised on 5 August 1914, the day after the outbreak of war. Even the Hunts Cycle Battalion was brought up to full strength on 11 August, although the unit was not sent to France until July 1916. People at home were not generally in physical danger during the First World War, although the *Hunts Post* recorded in January 1915 that preparations against hostile air-raids were being made.

R.A.F. Wyton, the first of seven service airfields in the county, was opened towards the end of the war. The land was sold off for agricultural purposes in 1918, but reopened in 1936. It is still in active use. Other R.A.F. bases, located at Somersham, Upwood and Warboys, were opened before or during the Second World War. Of these, only R.A.F. Upwood is still in military hands. The U.S. Airforce also built bomber airfields during the last war at Alconbury, Glatton and Molesworth. Only Alconbury is still actively used by American aircraft, although Molesworth has recently been reopened as a base for American nuclear missiles.

R.A.F. Wyton had the task of sending out a Blenheim bomber in September 1939, only hours after the outbreak of war, to make a reconnaissance flight over German ports. This was the first British operational sortie of the war. Huntingdonshire later became the headquarters of the 'Pathfinder' force, founded in August 1942, which had the task of lighting up night targets for bomber raids. Squadrons of this force were based at Wyton, Warboys, Graveley (on the border with Cambridgeshire), and Oakington near Cambridge. Two later squadrons, formed in May 1943, were based at Gransden and Bourn in Cambridgeshire. The headquarters of this force were moved in June 1943 from Wyton to Huntingdon; this is the reason why the headquarters of the Huntingdon District Council is called 'Pathfinder House'. The first local person to be killed was Arthur Flack of Earith in May 1940, who was a sailor on board a cruiser off the Norwegian coast. The Hunts Territorials, based in France, were evacuated from Dunkirk in June 1940.

The *Hunts Post* was full of articles about the effects of the black-out and the arrival of evacuees from London during the winter of 1939-40. One little boy, evacuated to Warboys, tried to return to London, and was finally tracked down after he had walked all the way to Hendon. People who stayed at home were certainly involved in the dangers of the last war to a far greater degree than had been the case in the First World War. In October 1940 an enemy aircraft crashed at Eaton Socon, killing all three crew members. During August 1941, 47 bombs fell on Huntingdon, causing extensive damage to property. One German bomber, returning from a raid over Peterborough during August 1942, discharged four high explosive bombs over Ramsey, killing seven people. This last incident was witnessed by Tim Hendley, then a small boy. He remembers finding a spent bullet lying on the floor of his father's garage—it had just missed the petrol tank of the family car. Other incidents occurred in 1944 when a plane crashed into a house at Tetworth, and in early 1945 when German 'fly-bombs' (as the *Hunts Post* called them) hit targets within the county. One hit Somersham, but there were no casualties. The *Hunts Post* revealed towards the end of the war that an estimated 567 high explosive bombs, and 4,468 incendiaries had landed within Huntingdonshire before the end of 1943. Most of these raids apparently went unrecorded because of censorship imposed on the newspaper.

The Disappearance of Huntingdonshire

Huntingdonshire disappeared as a county on 1 April 1974. This was not the first time that changes had been made to the old county boundaries. Slight alterations to tidy up anomalies were made in 1888, mainly dealing with detached or divided parishes. Swineshead was transferred to Bedfordshire in exchange for Tilbrook, while the portion of Winwick in Northamptonshire was transferred to Huntingdonshire. Luddington, Lutton and Thurning were all finally separated from the county. The former county boundary used to run through the centre of Thurning village. The detached portion of Tetworth, in the south of the county, was transferred to Bedfordshire more recently, in 1965. In the same year, Huntingdonshire was combined with the soke of Peterborough to form an enlarged county. The soke, once part of Northamptonshire, had enjoyed an independent existence since 1888. In 1974 Huntingdonshire and the soke of Peterborough were finally merged with Cambridgeshire and the Isle of Ely, the entire new county being known as Cambridgeshire.

The Huntingdonshire County Council therefore disappeared as a body in 1974. It was replaced by the Huntingdon District Council, which functions as

92 *John Major, MP for Huntingdon, with local constituents.*

a unit within the enlarged county of Cambridgeshire. The boundaries of the H.D.C. are very similar to those of the former county of Huntingdonshire. It is good to know that the H.D.C. has, within recent years, altered its title to the 'Huntingdonshire District Council'.

A few reminders that the Huntingdonshire area has not always been part of Cambridgeshire can be seen throughout the former county today. An old Huntingdonshire road-sign now graces the outside wall of the *Pheasant Inn* at Keyston. The town of Huntingdon retains a separate record office for county and parish documents dating before 1974. Several local societies, such as the Beds and Hunts Naturalists Trust, refuse to drop the old county name from their titles. It is to be hoped that the knowledge that there was once a county of Huntingdonshire will survive at least one more decade into the future.

Select Bibliography

Journals

Proceedings of the Cambridgeshire Antiquarian Society, vols.48 (1954), 52 (1958), 54 (1960), 58-62 inclusive (1965-9), 63 (1971), 65 (1974), 68-70 inclusive (1978-80)

Articles from *Records of Huntingdonshire* are cited under the appropriate headings below with the abbreviation *R.H.*

Prehistoric and Roman Huntingdonshire

Taylor, A., *Prehistoric Cambridgeshire*, 1977

Browne, D.M., *Roman Cambridgeshire*, 1977

Painter, K.S., 'The Water Newton Early Christian Silver', British Museum, 1977

Phillips, C.W. (ed.), 'The Fenland in Roman Times', *Royal Geographical Society Research Series*, no.5, 1970

Wild, J.P., 'The Romans in the Nene Valley', *Nene Valley Research Committee*, n.d.

Saxon, Norman and Medieval Huntingdonshire

Darby, H.C., *Medieval Cambridgeshire*, 1977

Hart, C.R., *The Early Charters of Eastern England*, 1966

Hatcher, J., 'Plague, Population and the English Economy, 1348-1530', *The Economic History Society*, 1977

Knowles, D., and Hadcock, R.N., *Medieval Religious Houses of England and Wales*, 1971

Mackreth, D.F., 'The Saxons in the Nene Valley', *Nene Valley Research Committee*, n.d.

Morris, J. (gen. ed.), *Domesday Book: Huntingdonshire*, 1975

Raftis, J.A., *The Estates of Ramsey Abbey*, 1957

Raftis, J.A., 'Social structures in five East Midland villages', *Economic History Review*, 1965

Raftis, J.A. and Hogan, M.P., *Early Huntingdonshire Lay Subsidy Rolls*, 1976

Stranks, C.J., *St Etheldreada, Queen and Abbess*, 1975

Savage, A. (ed.), *The Anglo-Saxon Chronicles*, 1982

Taylor, A., *Anglo-Saxon Cambridgeshire*, 1978

Usher, D., *Two Studies of Medieval Life*, 1953

Wise, J. and Noble, W.M., *Ramsey Abbey*, 1881

Tudor and Stuart Huntingdonshire

Banks, C.E., *Topographical Dictionary of English Emigrants to New England 1620-1650*, 1963
Bryant, A., *Samuel Pepys: the Man in the Making*, 1967
Camden, W., *Visitation of the County of Hunts in 1613* (ed. Sir H. Ellis), 1849
Fraser, A., *Cromwell, Our Chief of Men*, 1974
Maycock, A.L., *Nicholas Ferrar of Little Gidding*, 1963
Noble, W.M., *Huntingdonshire and the Spanish Armada*, 1896
Pepys, S., *Diaries*, ed. Matthews, W. and Latham, R.C., 1970 et seq.

1700 to the Present Day

Blakesef, C., *Elementary Education in Nineteenth-Century Huntingdonshire*, 1968
Cobbett, W., *Rural Rides*, 1822
Cox, T., *History of Huntingdonshire*, 1730
Defoe, D., *A Tour through the whole Island of Great Britain (1724-6)* (ed. P. Rogers), 1971
Hyde, H.A., *The Warboys Baptists*, 1963
Huntingdonshire County Handbook, 1963
Huntingdonshire: The Last 100 Years, 1990
Huntingdon District Official Guide, 1982
Kelly's Directories of Huntingdonshire, 1877, 1898, 1940

The Fenland

Darby, H.C., *The Draining of the Fens*, 1956
Dring, W.E., *The Fenland Story*, 1967
Godwin, H., *Fenland: its ancient past and uncertain future*, 1978
Storey, E., *Portrait of the Fen Country*, 1971

Towns and Great Houses

Bull, F., 'The impact of railways on St Ives', *R.H.*, 1983
Bull, F., *The Development of Markets and Market Functions in 19th-century Huntingdonshire*, 1982
Burkett, P.R., *Kimbolton Castle*, n.d.
Dickinson, P.G.M. et al., *A History of St Ives Rural District Council*, 1974
Dickinson, P.G.M., *Royal Charters of Huntingdon*, 1955
Dickinson, P.G.M., *Great Paxton*, 1972
Dunn, C., *The Book of Huntingdon*, 1977
Eaglen, R.J., 'The Mint at Huntingdon', *R.H.*, 1980
Green, H.J.M., *Godmanchester*, 1977
Hardwick, R.T., 'Huntingdon Town Hall', *R.H.*, 1982
Sweeney, M.M., *A History of Buckden Palace*, 1981
Tebbs, H.F., *Peterborough*, 1979
Tebbutt, C.F., *St Neots*, 1978

Agriculture and Enclosure

Burton, C.G., 'Sir R. Bernard and the Enclosure of Grafham', *R.H.*, 1983

Gray, II.L., *The English Field Systems*, 1915

Maxwell, G., *General View of the Agriculture of the County of Huntingdon, and Observations on the Means of its Improvement*, 1793

Meyer, W., 'Driving the Irish', *R.H.*, 1981

Parkinson, R., *General View of the Agriculture of the County of Huntingdon, Drawn up for the Consideration of the Board of Agriculture and Internal Improvement*, 1811

Porter, S., 'The Livestock Trade in Huntingdonshire, 1600-1750', *R.H.*, 1982

Stone, T., *General View of the Agriculture of the County of Huntingdon, with Observations on the Means of its Improvement*, 1793

General and Miscellaneous Works

Bigmore, P., *The Bedfordshire and Huntingdonshire Landscape*, 1979

Eliot, T.S., *Four Quartets*, 1944

Gelling, M., *Signposts to the Past*, 1978

Heseltine, P., *The Brasses of Huntingdonshire*, 1987

Hopewell, J., *Pillow Lace and Bobbins*, 1975

Kaminkow, J. and M., *A List of Emigrants from England to America 1718-1759*

Mawer, A. and Stenton, F., *The Place-Names of Bedfordshire and Huntingdonshire*, 1926

Mee, A., *The King's England: Bedfordshire and Huntingdonshire*, 1973 edition, edited by P. Dickinson

Spufford, M., *Contrasting Communities*, 1974

Victoria County History of Huntingdonshire, 1926

Index

Abbotsley, 32, 33, 85
Abbots Ripton, 32, 42, 79, 125, 127
Aboyne, Earls of, 101
Achurch, 65
Alconbury, 20, 21, 29, 32-34, 42-44, 90-1, 120, 134
Alconbury Weston, 32, 33, 131
Aldwinkle, 101
Alphery, Mikipher, 73, 107
Alwalton, 32, 43, 60, 129
Apreece family, 68, 75, 101
Apreece, Robert, 68, 75
Astwood, James and John, 85

Baker, Rev., 73
Barham, 32, 33
Barriss, John, 80
Barton, William, 95
Bayes, Thomas, 85
Beard, Dr. Thomas, 65
Bedell, Capell, 76
Bedell, Joseph, 73
Bedford, 29, 93-4, 107, 128
Bedford, Earl of, 76-7, 120
Bernard family, 102
Bernard, Sir Robert, 118
Berridge, John, 109
Birmingham, 91
Blisworth, 125
Bluntisham, 25, 32, 43, 108, 110, 111
Boddington, William, 123
Boston, 47
Bourn, 135
Bowen, Emanuel, 90, 100, 101
Bower, George, 88
Bowland, Anthony, 82, 83
Brampton, 18, 32, 40, 42, 64, 81, 82, 85, 99, 100-102, 114, 118, 133
Braughton, John, 92-3
Briggs, Joseph, 123
Brington, 32, 95
Broughton, 29, 32, 40, 64
Brown, John, 86
Brown, Lancelot 'Capability', 103, 104
Brown, L.R., 120
Browne, Robert, 65
Buckden, 17, 18, 25, 32, 59-61, 69, 91, 92, 109, 113, 126, 127, 131, 133
Buckworth, 32, 33, 43, 80, 101, 123

Bull, Thomas, 81
Bullen, John and Christmas, 123
Bullimore, Mr., 132
Bullock Road, 20-1, 29, 79, 91
Bunyan, John, 107
Bury, 32, 35, 52, 54, 64
Bythorn, 32, 85

Caldecote, 32, 43
Cambridge, 25, 35, 47, 50-52, 70, 72, 75, 77, 91, 102, 120, 126, 127, 131
Campion, Edmund, 68
Car Dyke, 25, 27
Carysfoot see Proby family
Castor, 26
Chatteris, 40, 108
Cheney, William, 123
Chesterton, 26, 29, 32, 64, 100, 101
Cirencester, 29
Clare, John, 119
Clifton family, 100
Cobbett, William, 87, 105
Colchester, 35
Colne, 28, 30, 32, 33, 114, 124
Conington, 20, 32, 51, 59, 62, 100, 101, 120
Coppingford, 29, 32, 42, 49, 106
Cottenham, 99
Cotton family, 62, 76, 85, 100, 101
Cotton, Sir Robert, 62
Coventry, 47
Covington, 32, 101, 114
Cowper, William, 105
Cresseuuelle, hundred of, 37
Cromwell, Henry, 102, 105
Cromwell, Sir Henry, 63
Cromwell, Margaret, 71
Cromwell, Oliver, 58, 59, 63, 65, 70-2, 99
Cromwell, Sir Oliver, 63, 70
Cromwell, Richard, 63
Cromwell, Robert, 70
Cromwell, Thomas, 63
Cromwell family, 63-5, 100-2, 116

Dawson, John, 129
Day, William, 92
Dean, 21, 32, 39
Defoe, Daniel, 78, 87, 92, 95
Denne, Henry, 107, 111

Denton, 32, 43, 52, 62, 101
Denver, 77
Dickinson, William, 68
Diddington, 32, 82, 85, 120
Dryden, John and family, 100
Duberley, W., 120
Dunscombe family, 101, 120
Durobrivae, 25-28, 30
Dyer, Sir James and Sir Richard, 100

Earith, 25, 28, 32, 33, 43, 74, 77, 78, 81, 90, 108, 124, 135
Easton, 32, 33, 82, 83, 114, 118
Eaton Ford, 25, 133
Eaton Socon, 17, 84, 133, 135
Eayre, Joseph, 87
Edinburgh, 91
Eliot, T.S., 67-8
Ellington, 29, 32, 35, 41, 55, 84, 100, 118
Elmes, James, 84
Elton, 18, 32, 38, 43, 44, 48, 49, 52, 62, 68, 81, 85, 101, 112, 120, 129
Ely, 31, 34, 42, 51, 53, 54, 58, 60, 61, 70, 71, 74, 80, 126
Ermine Street, 29, 37, 49, 90-1
Essom, Thomas, 124
Everton, 109
Eynesbury, 25, 32, 33, 43, 58, 60, 101

Faber, Rev. F.W., 112
Farcet, 28, 32, 101, 113
Feareflaxe, William, 90
Fellowes, Coulson, 102
Fellowes, Edward, 102, 120
Fellowes family, 116
Fengate, 18
Fenstanton, 17, 25, 32, 43, 60, 103, 107, 108
Fenton, 32, 33
Ferrar, John, 68, 69
Ferrar, Nicholas, 66-9, 73, 84, 95
Ferrar family, 84, 101
Fitzpier family, 44
Fitzwilliam family, 118, 120
Flack, Arthur, 135
Fletton, 32, 60, 101, 123, 126-8, 130, 131
Folksworth, 32, 113
Fox, George, 108

Gains Hall, 101
Glasgow, 91
Glatton, 32, 43, 45, 95, 101, 113, 124, 131, 134
Godmanchester, 17, 18, 22-6, 30, 32, 37, 46, 55, 57, 60, 85, 90, 96, 108, 109, 112-15, 122, 126, 128, 132, 133
Goslin, William, 90
Grafham, 32, 101, 114, 118, 126
Grafham Water, 29, 132
Gransden, 135
Grant, Thomas, 123
Graveley, 134
Graves, Robert, 79
Great Catworth, 32, 33, 38, 70, 85, 101, 123
Great Gidding, 29, 32, 33, 40, 43, 44, 108, 110, 118-19, 132
Great Gransden, 21, 42, 72, 79, 107, 110, 113, 120

Great North Road, 79, 90-2, 131
Great Paxton, 32-4, 88
Great Raveley, 32, 54, 64, 94
Great Staughton, 29, 32, 42, 46, 63, 71, 100, 114, 118, 120
Great Stukeley, 29, 32
Gunning, John, Mary and Elizabeth, 102-3

Haddock, Ralph, 68
Haddon, 32, 60
Hail Weston, 32, 104, 110
Halles, William, 65
Hamerton, 32, 42, 73, 76, 77, 123
Hammond family, 101
Hampton, J., 91
Handasy family, 101
Hardwicke, Lord, 102-3
Hargrave, 32
Hartford, 32, 50, 52, 54, 114, 118
Harthay, 42
Harvey, Thomas, 86
Hatfield, John, 123
Hawkins, Richard, 85
Heathcote, John M., 120
Hemingford Abbots, 17, 32, 38, 108, 133
Hemingford Grey, 32, 38, 47, 50, 52, 101, 102, 108, 114, 133
Hendley, Tim, 135
Hennesay, Tom, 91
Herbert, George, 66, 67
Hereford, 47
Hilton, 60, 103, 106
Hinchingbrooke, 45, 57, 58, 63, 64, 70, 98, 99, 100, 101, 115, 120
Holbeach, Laurence, 55
Holcroft, Thomas, 107
Holland, Earl of, 75
Holme, 32, 41, 43, 44, 94, 95, 113, 120, 124, 126
Holywell, 32, 49, 62, 101
Hopkinson, John, 129
Hopkinson, William, 105
Horner, William, 123
Horsey Hill, 74
Houghton, 18, 25, 32, 49, 50, 62, 114, 118, 122
Hughes, William, 123
Huntingdon, 17, 24, 32, 35, 37, 42, 43, 45-51, 55, 58, 59, 65, 70-5, 81, 86-8, 90-2, 95, 99, 104-10, 112-16, 119, 125-136.
Huntley, Marquis of, 120
Hurstingstone, hundred of, 29, 31, 36, 37, 54, 63, 111
Hussey, Richard H., 120

Jackson, John, 77, 100, 104
Jewson, George, 90
Johnson, Mr., 73
Johnson, Thomas, 86
Johnson, William, 84

Kaye, Bishop, 60
Kentish, Eustace, 104
Kettering, 126
Key, Edward, 96

Keysoe, 32, 33
Keyston, 32, 101, 136
Kimbolton, 21, 32-34, 37, 44, 47, 59, 63, 64, 69, 71, 84, 88, 90, 97, 98, 100, 101, 110, 111, 114, 115-117, 120, 126
King, Jasper, 86
Kings Lynn, 47, 71, 74, 77
Kings Ripton, 54, 100, 108
Kingston, Edward, 81
Kitson, Judith, 109

Lancaster, Thomas, 73
Laud, Archbishop, 65-66
Lea, Edward, 80-1
Leete, William, 85
Leicester, 20, 29, 47
Leighton Bromswold, 32, 36, 37, 43, 64, 66, 67, 84, 100, 113
Leightonstone, hundred of, 37, 63, 111
Lincoln, 25, 47, 60, 68, 75
Little Gidding, 32, 49, 67-9, 73, 101, 102, 129
Little Paxton, 17, 18, 25, 32, 33, 111, 120, 133
Little Raveley, 32, 35, 41, 64, 101
Little Stukeley, 32, 65, 114, 118
London, 25, 47, 52, 63, 66, 70, 71, 73, 79, 80, 90, 91, 95, 97, 99, 112, 120, 124, 126, 127, 133, 135
Longthorpe, 22, 26
Luddington, 32, 33, 135
Lutton, 135

Maddock, Rev. Matthew, 104
Major, John, 105, 136
Manchester, 2nd Earl of, 71, 72, 74, 98, 99, 107
Manchester, Earls and Dukes of, see Montagu family
Mandeville, Geoffrey de, 55
March, 90
Marshall, James, 61
Maxey, 18
Maxwell, George, 78, 84, 117, 121
Maycock, A.L., 67
Midloe, 111
Mills, John R., 120
Mitchell family, 101, 102
Mitchell, William, 102
Molesworth, 32, 33, 52, 64, 134
Monks Hardwick, 25, 108, 111
Monks Wood, 28, 106
Montagu, Edward, 64, 99, 100
Montagu, Sir Henry, 64
Montagu, Sidney, 64, 99
Montagu family, 63, 65, 87, 88, 90, 98-105, 115, 120, 128
Morborne, 32, 60
Mordaunt, Mrs., 68
Moyne, Sir William, 49

Neale, Edward, 80
Needingworth, 32, 108
Newman, John, 80
Noble, Mark, 86
Norman Cross, 37, 63, 101, 111, 128, 129
Norris, William, 79
Northampton, 47

Nye, Philip, 65

Oakington, 135
Offord Cluny, 18, 32, 60, 68, 114
Offord Darcy, 18, 32, 64, 68, 81, 84, 114
Old Hurst, 29, 32-34, 37, 101, 122
Old Weston, 32, 123
Oley, Barnabas, 72, 107
Orton Longueville, 18, 27, 30, 32, 101, 115, 116, 125
Orton Waterville, 18, 32, 60, 118, 122, 125
Oundle, 52
Overstone, Lord, 120
Oxford, 74

Paine, James, 88, 111
Papworth, 32
Parnell, John, 95
Parrish, Judith, 85
Pasheller, John, 95
Pegg, William, 86
Pelly, Sir Henry, 120 ·
Pepys, Pall, 100
Pepys, Paulina, 99
Pepys, Samuel, 59, 81, 97, 99-101
Perkins, John, 95
Pertenhall, 32
Peterborough, 27, 31, 35, 37, 53, 60, 62, 69, 95, 118, 120, 125-7, 129, 135
Philbrick, Thomas, 85
Pidley, 32, 80
Pigot family, 101
Pointer, John, 65
Pondersbridge, 124
Proby, Granville, 129
Proby, John, 101
Proby family, 101, 102, 120
Pryme, Charles de la, 120
Pym, Francis, 120

Quincey, William, 123

Ramsey, 20, 34, 40, 43, 44, 46, 47, 48-9, 53-8, 60, 62-4, 77, 84, 89, 90, 94, 101, 102, 113, 115, 116, 120, 123, 124, 126, 128, 132, 134, 135
Reading, 56
Renton, David, 105
Reynolds, Edward, 120
Robertson, Charles, 120
Rowley, G.W., 120
Russell, Bishop, 60
Rust, James, 120

St Albans, 56
St Ives, 17, 18, 25, 31-4, 44-7, 49, 50-1, 53, 54, 57-8, 65, 70-2, 74, 85, 86, 88-90, 94, 101, 10811, 114, 116, 121-3, 126-8, 130-4
St John family, 100
St Neots, 17, 25, 33, 46, 50, 58, 62, 64, 74, 75, 84, 86-8, 92-6, 101, 109-12, 114-17, 120, 128, 132-4
Sanderson, Bishop, 60
Sandy, 22, 25, 120

Sandwich, Earls of, *see* Montagu
Sapcote family, 101
Sapley, 32, 42
Savage, Hayes, 123
Savage, John, 95
Savidge, Rev., 73-4
Sawtry, 26, 28, 32, 41, 49, 51, 55, 59, 60, 62-3, 76, 80, 81,
    101, 114, 116, 123, 133
Selby, 56
Sherborne, 52
Sibson, 27, 32, 60
Slepe *see* St Ives
Smith-Barry, A.H., 120
Somersham, 20, 28, 31-4, 42, 43, 54, 60, 61, 79, 101, 114,
    124, 126, 133-5
Southoe, 32
Southwark, 52
Spaldwick, 31, 32, 34, 44, 60, 64, 101, 110, 114, 118
Sparrow, Olivia Bernard, 102
Speed, John, 42, 59, 88, 90, 105
Spencer, Arnold, 94
Squire, Bartholomew, 84
Stamford, 47, 65, 95
Stanground, 27, 32, 41, 60, 62, 74, 113, 115, 116, 132
Steeple Gidding, 29, 32, 44, 62, 76, 85, 101, 123, 133
Stevenson, Samuel, 86
Stibbington, 32, 60, 114, 125
Stilton, 32, 44, 74, 92-3, 101, 118, 131
Stirtloe, 25, 111
Stone, Phillip, 71
Stone, Thomas, 78, 92, 117, 121
Stonely, 59
Stow Longa, 32, 33, 34, 101, 114
Streets, Edward, 86
Swineshead, 32, 33, 101, 135
Sylvester, Nathaniel, 85

Tabard, John, 40
Taylard, William, 64
Taylor, Ann, 68
Tetworth, 32, 44, 68, 135
Thorney, 60
Thornhill, George, 120
Thrapston, 26
Throssel, Francis and William, 108
Thurning, 32, 33, 44, 60, 135
Tilbrook, 32, 38, 39, 49, 73, 135
Titus, Colonel, 102
Torkington, L.J., 120
Toseland, 32, 33, 37, 63, 111, 114
Tubbs, Mr., 78

Upthorpe, 35
Upton, 32, 34, 101, 106, 123, 129
Upwood, 29, 32, 54, 64, 100, 115, 120, 134

Venn, Henry and John, 110
Vermuyden, Cornelius van, 77

Wakefield, Stephen, 68
Walton, George, 63, 70
Walton, Valentine, 70-1
Wansford, 32, 92, 105, 126, 127
Warboys, 20, 32, 40, 64, 84, 107-9, 111, 114, 123, 127, 131,
    134, 135
Waresley, 32, 120
Washingley, 32, 38, 49, 68, 101, 120
Water Newton, 22, 24, 25, 27, 28, 32, 60, 84
Waverley, 59
Webb, Theodore, 120
Wells, Dr., 65
Wells, William, 120
Welstead, J.R., 120
Wesley, John, 77-8, 109
Westminster, 62, 68
Weybridge, 42
White, John, 129
Whittlesey, 74
Whittlesey Mere, 41, 57, 59, 77, 78, 106, 123, 132
Wilberforce, William, 101
Williams, Bishop John, 60, 65
Williams (alias Cromwell) family, 63, 101
Winchester, 47
Wingfield, Sir Edward, 63
Wingfield family, 100
Winter, James, 86
Winwick, 32, 33, 38, 84, 95, 108, 135
Wisbech, 126
Wistow, 29, 32, 34, 35, 54, 64, 68, 73, 80, 82
Woodhurst, 29, 32, 33, 114, 122
Woodstone, 32, 44, 130
Wood Walton, 20, 29, 32, 47, 51, 55, 59, 78-80
Woolley, 32, 73, 107
Wright, William, 123
Wyton, 29, 32, 118, 134, 135

Yaxley, 20, 28, 32, 37, 44, 60, 62, 82, 83, 86, 94, 101, 110,
    123, 126, 129, 132
Yelling, 38, 79, 81, 82, 110, 114
Yewle, Richard, 79
York, 25, 47, 90, 127
Young, Arthur, 117
Young, William, 79, 81